SPA

TOMORROW

An Unexpected Life-Changing Journey

BOB ABLE

Second Edition

For David and Carol, to whom we always seem to owe so much; and of course Bee and Milly, who made it all possible.

CONTENTS

Contacts and Links

EMAIL: bobable693@gmail.com

FACEBOOK: Bob Able

INSTAGRAM: BobAbleAuthor

WEBSITE:
https://bobable693.wixsite.com/spaintomorrow

CHAPTER 1: WHAT A SURPRISE!

So what do you do when your loveable but slightly batty mother-in-law unexpectedly leaves you not quite enough money to change your life?

Having retired early with a pension that promised jam tomorrow but delivered only enough to fill the occasional doughnut, my life revolved around looking after my very sprightly, but very elderly, mother and supporting Bee, my wife, to regularly rescue my erratic, often irascible, and entirely eccentric mother-in-law from her latest disaster. We certainly didn't expect to inherit anything.

Following the cost of an urgent downsizing house move, necessitated by her revelation that she had almost run out of money, and shortly afterwards by her admission into an eye-wateringly expensive nursing home in commuter belt Surrey, mother-in-law, or Milly, as I affectionately called her, passed away. After such expense Bee and I were therefore very surprised to learn that each of Milly's four daughters was to receive a modest inheritance.

Until this point, one of the issues with my version of early retirement, bought on by back problems, the worldwide financial crash, and the fact that my company had acquired a competitor and didn't need two of me, was that my responsibilities in terms of caring for my mother didn't allow me to throw myself into anything terribly absorbing.
So, as so many do and to keep myself out of the pub, I turned on the TV.
And I watched enthralled as people not unlike me bought holiday homes in the sun with consummate ease for seemingly bargain prices and looked forward to a joyful retirement in sunnier climes.

Dreaming was at least free.

Previously, before Milly died, Bee and I had been looking at ways to increase our income and had become disappointed that, after finally managing to sell our money pit of a house and move to something smaller, we still couldn't afford to buy a second property and join the ranks of the buy-to-let landlords. When Milly died, however, we were able to have a rethink.

Bee, my wife of thirty years, worked in a nursery school, first as a teacher, then a teaching assistant and finally, through a bizarre set of circumstances, as the school cook. That meant we always had to take our breaks in the school holidays, even when both our boys grew up and one had a home of his own.

Inevitably then, our holidays always had to be taken at the most expensive time of the year, and our finances dictated that the world tour was never going to be on the agenda. My mother was infirm and very dependent, so we'd never allowed ourselves a long break either. But now everything had changed.

During Milly's last weeks and months, Bee and her sisters had taken over Milly's finances and arrangements completely.. But nursing care, especially for those with dementia in leafy Surrey, is terrifyingly expensive. We hoped that, when the time came, there would be enough to pay the funeral expenses. We also hoped what money she had would last as long as she did.

Imagine our surprise then, when it came to the reckoning and the lawyers had extracted their considerable chunk of the cake and following the quite rapid sale of Milly's retirement flat, that there was a sum of money left over.

It wasn't enough to buy that second home to rent out, even where we lived on the east coast in darkest Norfolk, but it certainly helped and gave us pause for thought as to what to do with the money for the best.
Our finances, having convinced the Church of England to take our vast money pit of a house that Bee hated off our hands and turn it into a vicarage, and bought a modern box on an estate without a mortgage, were on a firmer footing when the inheritance came through. We hoped to be able to move to the point where Bee could soon retire, but with post-crash interest rates on the floor, we weren't going to do well if we just invested the money in the bank, and we felt some urgency to do something with it.

It wasn't long before I was hooked on those TV programmes about overseas property and started to look into it seriously.

There were brochures to be read, a visit to an overseas property exhibition in London, and all the fun of the fair. I even convinced Bee that we should go for a short break to one of the locations I rather fancied. Just for a look, you understand.
None of this was going to be possible without the

money from Milly, of course, and that money was Bee's; so the decision as to what, if anything, to do with it wasn't mine.

But Bee had watched a few of the TV programmes too and, whilst not convinced, she was at least intrigued. So we decided to go and have a look.

The spot chosen for our visit, just for a look, you understand, was a small working town in Spain on the Costa Blanca, or white coast, called Almazara. It wasn't so much of a tourist hotspot and wasn't overrun with Brits in Union Jack swimming trunks like some areas of southern Spain. It was however on the coast and did have a reputation as a 'town of gastronomy' which, given how keen I am on my food, was a draw in itself.

We'd been offered, and resisted, all sorts of free or discounted inspection trips to other more typically expat areas, but there was nothing like that available in Almazara, and that in itself was a major attraction for us.
Could this be as close as you could get to 'proper Spain' on the coast, albeit with the dreadful spectre of Benidorm just over an hour down the motorway to provide a blot on the sunny horizon.

It couldn't be like that really, could it?

It would be all beer, chips, and all-day breakfasts just like so many ruined coastal Spanish places.

Many people like that sort of thing, and good luck to them; but it's not for us.

I'm sure you can find fish and chips on the menu if you look hard enough anywhere, but there was no sign of the Union Jacks and Sunday roasts in Almazara. The expat population was a modest percentage of the whole and from all over Europe and beyond. There were Brits, of course, but not that many.

It wasn't a rural backwater inhabited by straw chewing yokels, but it wasn't a sell-out either.

This part of Spain, the Marina Alta, is much more verdant than the more southern Costas. Being closer to Valencia than Malaga makes the flora almost entirely different too. Bougainvillea, oleander, and hibiscus flower on every corner, but there are groves of oranges, avocados, almonds, and vines everywhere, and seas of fragrant orange blossom vie for the title of dominant species with the inevitable olives and vines.
The landscape here is predominantly green and never becomes quite as parched as the south.
The houses are mostly white or a sort of cream, interspersed here and there with the odd pink or brown one, but exposed brickwork is rare and high rises nonexistent.

My research showed the climate in this spot is also more temperate. The winters are delightfully

mild, but the summers don't get quite as scorchingly hot as a rule. Obviously it rains more frequently to keep everything so green, but the Internet proclaimed that the air
quality was some of the best in Europe, and with little light pollution, that the black night skies reveal the firmament in all its glory..... Well then, what was the harm in going to have a look for ourselves?

Start packing, Bee!

◆ ◆ ◆

CHAPTER 2: JUST FOR A LOOK, YOU UNDERSTAND

In the UK Bee and I had bought houses on mortgages and done up wrecks in our efforts to increase our equity just as everyone else does, but we'd never bought a property outright and for cash, and the prospect was daunting. In addition, these properties were in a foreign country where we didn't even speak the language. Bee had always said she saw no point in holidaying in the same place twice, so there was certainly going to be a mountain to climb.

But we were here in Spain now. Just for a look, you understand.
What could it hurt to go and look at the outside of that place on a mountain with terrific views we found on the Internet? Have hire car, will travel.

So we phoned the agent, who turned out to be German, and we were very surprised by what happened next.
We met at the entrance to a rather grand private estate with gate houses and security guards, and with his 'You follow...' we assumed that he would lead us from there to a more modest location nearby.

But he drove straight into the estate past the security guards, giving them a wave, and on past huge sprawling villas with pools and tennis courts (and even, we learned later, one with a helipad) built into the side of the mountain, all looking towards the Med.

Perhaps this was a shortcut to the more modest houses, or maybe the agent used this route to dazzle punters before introducing the reality.
I was wrong.
'Surely the property's not actually on this private estate, next door to the millionaires' villas,' I whispered to Bee behind my hand.
'Good heavens,' exclaimed Bee. 'There are pockets of apartments right on this spectacular mountain.'
'Perhaps they were built for the servants of the people in those mansions,' I joked.

Of course the agent had the keys in his pocket. He would have, wouldn't he.

'The inside can't possibly be as nice as the outside in this sort of location,' I muttered, as we got out of our car. 'And for this sort of money, it's probably a wreck.'

'At least if we go in, we can say we've been,' she replied. 'Then we can put this silly dream to bed without those nagging "what if" doubts.'
'OK, let's have a look inside.'

As we walked up the entrance steps, the agent explained. 'Further steps lead down to the private underground garage we'll see in a minute.'
Underground garage? Incredible, I thought.
After a struggle to find the right key, the agent opened the front door.

I opened one eye.
Then both eyes.
Wide!

So far it was lovely. A spacious well-decorated marble tiled hall with quality wooden doors to each of the rooms and a wide archway to the lounge. But it was pitch dark.
This wouldn't do at all.
Hang on. The agent was pulling a little rope.
The steel blinds rose, and sunlight flooded in.
I was flabbergasted.

There was a mistake, of course. It was the language

barrier. The German agent had surely misunderstood our price limit.
Are you sure this price is right?' I asked hesitantly, glancing at the details.
The agent looked sheepish. 'Yes, this is the asking price. But the owner, he will consider the lower offer, if you like.'
Like! I was enchanted, and as each room was revealed, it got progressively better. Even Bee had to admit she was impressed.

The agent took us to see the two swimming pools, shared with just 30 other properties and not for public use, and the underground garage.
'That's your garage,' the agent pointed. 'Next to the Lamborghini and to the right of the Maserati.'
No. Really? It even had an electrically operated door!

We nodded appreciatively as we were shown the secure private store containing two sets of golf clubs but big enough for a motorbike or two.
'Is that a golf course?' I asked, squinting into the sunshine.
'Yes. If you go over the private road, down the hill at the end of the landscaped gardens, there's a 27-hole golf course. Beyond that, off the estate and approached from a separate road, is a five star hotel containing a spa which has won 'best spa in Spain'. Twice.'

◆ ◆ ◆

In order to steady ourselves, we went around the apartment again and, from the balcony, admired the views of the Med, which was about five minutes away by car, beyond the golf course, and the adjacent mountain nature reserve.

On the way out, we followed the agent past the tennis club ... 'Very 'sclusive,' he said. 'Two famous professional coaches' ... and the horse-riding stables, until he left us at the entrance by the security guard's station.

Blimey!

◆ ◆ ◆

CHAPTER 3: PARADISE FOUND?

Did I mention Brexit? Well, all that was going on while we were doing this.

Our first trip was before the Referendum, with the Prime Minister promising to deliver promptly on whatever the outcome was; confident that, as he saw it, common sense would prevail and the vote would be solidly to remain in the EU.

We thought that was what would happen too, so we continued to dream of our place in the sun and to plan for it.

Our second visit, however, was booked before, but taken after, the Referendum.

The spectacularly close vote had produced a victory for the 'Leave' camp by the tiniest margin.

The Prime Minister, despite his promise to see Brexit through to its conclusion, had resigned not only as PM but from politics altogether, and things were looking a lot more uncertain.

The winning 'Leave' group had promised that nothing would change; that we could enjoy all of the benefits of EU membership and be free to trade and travel wherever and whenever we wanted, as before. We knew that was nonsense, of course, but we didn't expect it to be as categorically wrong as it turned out, so we ploughed on.

'We shouldn't buy the first place we see, should we?' Bee and I debated.

So we arranged with a few other agents to view some different properties, including an apartment in the same block which was similar but lacked the style of the first one (and was more expensive). We also viewed a tiny terraced bungalow closer to the sea which was no bigger than a studio flat.

A little house in a village a few miles along the coast was nice, but turned out to be in a German expat enclave where chorizo had been replaced with bratwurst, and we viewed a few other lacklustre apartments elsewhere.

We met one charming and very knowledgeable agent who, unusually for this area, was Canadian. Unfortunately she didn't have the right property for us but she took us to some interesting places such as Montaña de Cielo, high up in the mountains.

In fact it was so high that for part of the time the properties were actually above the cloud line. What might have been a spectacular view out to sea was just a view of the top of the clouds and the occasional passing aircraft!

We took time to explore on our own in the hire car, without the agents, and discovered an equal proportion of pretty villages and towns and soul-less, semi-abandoned urbanisations where the de-velopers had gone bust and the banks had moved in. Spain's economic crisis was, in a sense, working to our advantage in that property prices had col-lapsed, with many offered at prices half of those before the crash. However the desolation in some places created by the often ill-considered actions of the banks, and the subsequent blight on invest-ment, was a depressing sight.

Even on our favourite urbanization, there were a few unsold plots waiting for a millionaire to build another magnificent villa, and at the bottom of the hill there was a small abandoned half-built project.

We learned that this little speculative develop-ment had been stopped because the builder hadn't actually bothered to secure any form of planning permission for it before offering the handful of luxury apartments with golf course views to the unsuspecting public, and putting up the concrete frame!

It presented a bleak facade now that it was locked up and abandoned. Nothing like the promises in the glossy brochure we glimpsed in one of the agent's offices, which showed opulent living for the well-heeled on the fairways.

While these broken dreams were slightly sad and contained a message for us to be cautious, the area we chose, higher up the mountain, was so well kept and prosperous looking (which was reflected in the comparatively high maintenance charges, of course) that we were undeterred.

We knew that sustainable quality like this was never going to come cheap but those maintenance charges did cover the two private pools, extensive landscaped grounds, exterior decoration, cleaning and insurance, as well as 24-hour security.
The charges were, however, a third less than my son paid on a small flat on the outskirts of Norwich back in the UK, so we could live with that.

It was clear that my assiduous Internet searching and homework into the area around the first apartment had proved accurate. That first one stood head and shoulders above everything else and, sensing a glimmer of interest, the agent told us that all the rather classy furniture could be included if we wanted it.

We arranged a second viewing, but Bee was still

unsure that she wanted to break her vow never to holiday in the same place twice.
'There is so much world out there to explore,' she said.
'Yes,' I replied, 'and we can use that place as a jumping-off point to explore some more. No doubt the flight taxes will be less too, if we start from Spain.'

We 'yes butted' and 'what iffed' for a while and agreed that with interest rates so low, and the uncertainties Brexit created, investing in the UK was probably no safer than investing in Spain.
'And,' I reasoned, 'we could always rent it out for holiday lets if we wanted to.'

Bee looked pensive but I drew a deep breath and delivered my coup de grâce.
'Milly would've loved this place,' I said as we prepared to drive away from the apartment for the second time.
I'd hit the spot. There was no doubt that Milly would have absolutely loved the area, the apartment, and the whole idea of a holiday home in Spain.

As a child, Bee had holidayed several times in a family friend's place near the beach in Tarragona on the Costa Brava. She and her mother had remembered these trips with great affection, and I could see there was a rich vein to be mined if I continued along this track.

Then Bee surprised me.

Over coffee, on the morning of the day we were due to fly home, she said, 'OK, let's do it. Let's make an offer!'

CHAPTER 4: READY?

I'd read everything I could lay my Kindle on about living in Spain. From the iconic, if idealised *Driving Over Lemons* by Chris Stewart to Yvonne Bartholomew's excellent *Dreaming of Retiring to the Costa Blanca? Read this First:* and absolutely everything Victoria Twead had written from *Chickens, Mules and Two Old Fools* onwards. This I had tempered with classic and harrowing tales of the Spanish Civil War, and life under Franco by various artists.

I'd joined a Spanish conversation group and then taken more formal Spanish lessons (not that much of it seems to have stuck) and tried my best to understand what we were letting ourselves in for. But more and more I became enchanted by the prospect of life in Spain, even if it was only as a tourist.

There is something remarkably relaxing about being in Spain. A sort of automatic contentment, which I didn't expect.

'You remember when we had that boat, Bee, and I always said that when you let go the ropes and we pulled away from the bank, peace invades?' I asked. 'Well, being in Spain is a bit like that.'

'Yes,' said Bee. 'But without the lifejackets!'

◆ ◆ ◆

The apartment we rented for a fortnight further down the mountain at the time of our second viewing was much nicer than the hotel by the beach where we stayed on our first visit and considerably cheaper. We'd found it through one of those websites people use to rent out their holiday homes.
We were met at the door by the owner's local representative who held the keys.

Peter Gunn was in his 70's and tall and lanky. He and his wife had moved to Spain fifteen years before from Hampshire. He was one of those capable individuals who knew someone who could fix anything and how everything worked. He settled us in and, as we unloaded the cases from the tiny hire car, chatted amiably asking why we were there and what our plans were.

When he discovered we were looking for property he offered a series of useful pieces of advice and some contacts to help us. It was the start of a long friendship and, to this day, we are grateful to Peter and his charming wife, Holly, for all they did for us. Peter told me that the apartment we had rented also happened to be for sale and, while it was not for us, he said he would see what else he could think of.

When we told him where the one we liked was, he confirmed that yes, that was a good location and probably the best place to buy for our budget.
It was all very encouraging.

Meanwhile the Pound was falling like a stone against the Euro as a result of the Brexit vote.
At the airports people were getting less than £1 for a Euro. Our timing couldn't have been worse.
Could this really be a good move for us?

◆ ◆ ◆

CHAPTER 5: STEADY

'We'd like to make our offer in Pounds Sterling, not Euros, please,' I told the agent.

'No problem, I'm sure the Irish owner in Belfast will be happy with that.' He said.
So, swallowing hard, we made a cheeky offer.
Nothing ventured......

It was refused immediately.

'The owners are very keen to sell,' the agent told us. 'But perhaps a little more...'
No further comment was made about our offer being in Pounds, unusual though that may have been, so we raised it by a couple of thousand and waited.
Later, as we were dusting off the cases to be ready to pack, the agent rang.

'Your revised offer still isn't acceptable,' he said.

'The owner stated a figure that they'll accept, without the furniture, for a quick sale. This is the figure you must pay if you want it.' And he mentioned the price.

We already knew that, even at the asking price, the apartment compared very favourably with others on the market, so we felt a little guilty offering low again. Only a little guilty though, and only for a minute!

We offered a couple of thousand less than the vendor's price, in Pounds, and to include all the furniture.

'It's our final offer,' we told him. 'It's all we can afford.'

'Well, I'll contact the owner and let you know what he says.'

What followed next was the first of several underhand tactics, bordering on downright dishonesty, that he employed.

'The offer might be acceptable if you paid me a deposit in cash now,' he suggested, 'and agreed to pay 10% of the price in cash as soon as the contract is drawn up, by my own solicitor, who you could use.'

We'd read about this sort of 'black money' fiddle where the price being paid and the price on the contract were not the same. It was gradually being clamped down on and was illegal in Spain, and indeed one of the other agents we'd spoken to had admitted that he'd personally been caught out on his own purchase when the tax authorities caught up with him.

I strongly believe that if you have a written record of a conversation you have something to fall back on if it goes wrong and, as a result, I started to negotiate by email, rather than over the phone.

Our offer, I wrote, was for the figure the vendor would now accept, in Pounds, but to include all the furniture and the two sets of golf clubs in the store, and was subject to a structural survey and contract.
I stated that I would use my own solicitor, thank you very much, and that all of the money would be passed through, or held by, him. There would be no cash payments and our lawyer (who Peter Gunn had kindly introduced us to in readiness) would expect a contract from the vendor's lawyers if the offer was acceptable.
I also stated that the agent should provide us with a detailed inventory of what was to be included in the sale, particularly as the apartment obviously contained some personal items, toiletries etc., which no doubt the current owners would like to remove.

It all went quiet.
As we were driving to the airport, a female assistant from the agent's office rang.
I held the phone away from my ear so that Bee could hear.
'Your offer has been accepted. Are you prepared to proceed?'
'Yes, of course we are!'
As I hung up I stopped the car and grabbed Bee's hand.
'Whaaahooo!' I let slip, 'We are going to buy a place in Spain!'
'Yes dear, and now we need to get home and sort the money out,' she laughed 'So come on, if we don't get to the airport in two hours we are going to miss the flight!'

The agent would never know we'd been discussing whether we could increase our offer, and now we didn't have to.

This was getting really exciting!

We called the solicitor and asked him to contact the agent for details to proceed and set off, just below the speed limit, of course, to catch that flight!

CHAPTER 6: STOP!

Back home and the wires were hot as emails flew backwards and forwards. We'd just had time to open a bank account before we left Spain, again thanks to an introduction from Peter Gunn to his own British-born bank manager, who was to prove invaluable as matters moved forward.

We also applied for the all-important N.I.E. number, without which nothing remotely financial moves in Spain. We traveled to the Spanish Consulate round the back of Harrods in London to sort this out in person.
It was a nice day out for us rural Norfolk types, even if the main purpose was only to acquire the Spanish equivalent of a Social Security number so that the Spanish Government could extract tax from us.

While we identified and appointed a British qualified structural surveyor and gave him the agent's number to arrange access, the lawyer established who their counterparts would be on the vendor's side and requested a contract.

Meanwhile the Pound continued to slide against the Euro and Brexit caused all sorts of panic in the UK as the Conservatives elected a new leader.

The only thing anyone outside Westminster had to say about our new PM at that stage was a comment made by Ken Clarke MP, describing her in an unguarded moment as a 'Bloody difficult woman.'

The Spanish solicitor, who spoke understandable English so long as you reminded him to slow down, introduced us to his assistant, Valentina, a charming young lady who spoke excellent English. She explained they'd started their work and asked for the first instalment of the fees.

Then, this being August in Spain, when everything stops, everything stopped.

Meanwhile the agent was a bit awkward about giving the key to the surveyor and refused to attend himself but eventually, after a few threats to withdraw on our part, he relented. The property passed with flying colours, and the surveyor produced an excellent report with photographs of every detail in just 24 hours.

But there was nothing happening on the legal front and although our lawyer's office remained open, it seemed the vendor's Spanish solicitor, who was also the one the agent had tried to get us to use, had packed up for the month of August, so that was that.
No amount of pushing on my part produced any response, and the agent kept not quite getting around to producing the inventory we required to make it clear what was to remain and was included in the sale.

The excuses the agent gave included trying to tell us there was no need for such a document because everything we'd seen was included; that this was quite normal in Spain, and that I hadn't paid him to produce the document.
The real reason, I suspect, was that his office was some miles away from the property and he couldn't be bothered to drive over.

The period of inactivity on the legal side did however allow us to get our financial arrangements sorted out and to find and appoint a currency exchange company to organise money transfers at a much cheaper cost than the banks. We were delighted to have been able to discuss our requirements with several of these organisations at the property exhibition we went to in London and had learned that the service they offered and the fees they charged varied considerably. We ended up using Smart Currency Exchange who were really helpful and even sent us a Spanish phrase book as a thank you for using their services.

CHAPTER 7: CAUTION

When August was over, the lawyers resumed hostilities. A contract emerged but there was still no sign of the inventory which was due to be included and prepared by the agent. The contract had the price in Euros and the agent denied all knowledge of being asked to make our offer in Pounds. The owner, seeing the Pound continue to slide, insisted it was Euros or nothing, even though he lived in the UK currency area.

Back in England I conducted email conversations on various aspects of the legal stuff as it emerged. I was probably considered a bit of a pain by our lawyer because, after a career in property development, covering the legal side of things, so long as the details were translated into English, I knew what I was looking at.

As a result I confess I bombarded them with questions where there were gaps in the legal title information and one point really bothered me.

It wasn't clear who owned the roads.

Many people had bought property over the years on this urbanisation without this issue causing problems, but to me it was a ticking time bomb. Eventually those roads were going to need repair and maintenance and, as it didn't seem to be anybody's responsibility to pick up the cost, I saw a major problem.
Despite assurances from the lawyer that all was well, I worried at this issue and wouldn't let it drop. I could see that this point had been missed or ignored over and over again, and I wasn't going to give in.

Eventually, somewhat unwillingly, our solicitor agreed to write on an official basis to the Local Authority and try to resolve the issue.

The agent and the owner's lawyer were not, of course, interested in helping and said it was for us to deal with if we wanted to.
What astonished me about this lack of attention to detail was that the owners of the apartment, and presumably many others, had mortgages on these places, so the banks were also at risk of having unsaleable property if the balloon went up.

At first the Town Hall offered a slightly mealy-mouthed response to our request, saying that they hadn't been asked to maintain the roads.
That didn't answer the question, which I insisted the lawyer repeated.
The question was whose responsibility was it to repair and maintain the roads and who did they belong to.

Eventually I got a call from our lawyer, which was an unusual occurrence in itself, with most of our interaction taking place by email.
'Señor Bob,' he said, 'it seem you have opened up the big problem. The Town Hall, they don't want to admit it, but they no have done the paperwork right when these houses built.'

Oh dear.

'Now we find the builder, he pay the Town Hall to take over the roads when they built, but the Council never finish the papers.'
'And the builder is long gone, I assume?' I asked him.
'No, he still in business. He still build the villas for if he sells building plots.'

'Well then, all that needs to be done is for the Town Hall and the builder to get together and sign the paperwork and the roads will belong to the Council!'.

'Yes, but...'
There had to be a but.

'The roads, they need some repairs and the drains also. The Town Hall say the builder must pay to put right.'
'So the builder doesn't fancy doing any further work because he's already paid the Council to take them over.'
'Sí, is very difficulty.'
'Have the Town Hall confirmed that they were paid by the builder?' I asked.
'They just found out they were, they say, but is not enough for to pay for the repairs now as ten years more go by.'

'So how are we to resolve this?'
'I want you give permission me to send letter to the Resident's Association to say them this happen. Maybe they force the Town Hall to do it.'
'D'you think that will work?'
'Sí, is very lucky. Mayor elections coming and the Mayor, he no want to tell this in the newspapers.'
'So it's the same Mayor who collected the money but didn't finish the paperwork?'
'Sí. Is big problem.'

I agreed that he could write to the Resident's Association but insisted that he sent a copy to the Mayor so that he would be on notice as to what was going on.

After a nervous wait, during which the owner's solicitors started to get threatening, saying we were delaying unnecessarily and refusing to acknowledge that there was a problem, the Town Hall relented and finalised the paperwork so that they were now responsible for the road maintenance and for doing the outstanding repairs.

I never did find out if the Mayor was re-elected, but I wouldn't be surprised if he was.
I did wonder if the owner's solicitors (who were also the same firm the agent wanted us to use) knew the Mayor and maybe that would explain why they made such a fuss over this.

Couldn't be, could it?

Spain is very different from the UK, it seems.

CHAPTER 8: GO!

We weren't the sort of people who did this sort of thing. It continually astonished me that we *were* doing it, and even now it amazes me that we *did* do it!
Yes, cursed with insatiable ambition, I'd previously climbed the corporate ladder, and yes, I ended up driving the firm's Mercedes, but my career was always precarious and I was only ever as good as my next deal.
That sort of pressure and uncertainty wears you down, and aspirations tend to revolve around looking forward to a quiet weekend, if there wasn't a tender submission to write or paperwork to catch up on. Certainly I hadn't expected to be looking forward to collecting the keys of our property in Spain.

Bee, after taking time out to raise our two boys and steadfastly rejecting the prospect of promotion for a calmer life, was the stable one. The foun-

dation on which our family's often rocky passage through life was built.
We should have been having a quiet retirement, with little more pressing to worry about than whether the camellia would flower this year and what to do about that bald patch of lawn.
How on earth did we end up queueing to board yet another Ryanair flight from a chilly Stanstead airport?!

But here we were, on the way to meet the lawyers and go to the Notary to finalise the deal.
The camellia and the dodgy patch of lawn were right down the bottom of our priority list, and we didn't give them a second thought as we shuffled through the cattle-class air gate once more.

Our days ahead involved collecting bank transfers and delivering them to the lawyers, checking arrangements to have water bills put in our name, and making sure the electricity was on.

At last there was some sign of the inventory. The agent, after being put under some pressure by our lawyer and eventually by the owners themselves, when I managed to get a message to them as to what was holding it up, had finally produced a scruffy hand-written single side of A4 which ignored most of the contents of the drawers and cupboards (presumably because he was too idle to open them) and made no mention of the golf clubs or anything in the store, so in the end I had the solicitors confirm to each other that they were included.

He'd dithered about at this for so long and been so obstructive about producing this document that we'd all but given up on it. His only contact with us was to try to persuade us to get a proportion of the completion monies from the bank in cash to cover his fees to be paid over to him personally on completion. Needless to say we resisted that robustly.

Trying to extract the inventory from him had frankly driven me to distraction.
'That's the fourth time you've mentioned that,' Bee scolded. 'Do stop worrying.'

'Ryanair Flight Fizz, Crackle, Squeak, now boarding at Gate Pop!'

Time for us to start a new chapter.

CHAPTER 9: DANCING WHILE WE WASH

Everything about the apartment looked great. The furniture was clearly not new, but was of excellent quality and must have been expensive.

OK, the bigger of the two cream leather sofas had discolouring on the lip of the seat.

'That's the effects of sun cream and sun,' said Bee knowledgeably, but other than that there seemed to be no other obvious damage.

'That ancient analogue TV will have to go,' I mused.

'I don't fancy that elderly microwave either,' said Bee. 'Let's get rid of some of the obvious stuff first though. This hairbrush looks gross for a start,' she said as she gingerly picked it up with the tips of her fingers and bagged it up to be binned later. 'You could just about make a wig from all the hair in it!'

'I can't wait to see if the two sets of golf clubs are still in the store,' I said, and rifled through the mountain of keys to find the right one. 'I don't expect much. They're probably old mis-matched clubs but maybe one or two could be salvaged.'
'See you in a while,' Bee said as congealed half-empty sun-cream bottles, toenail clippers, and dried-up soap the previous occupant had kindly left behind joined the hairy brush.
When the agent said everything in the place was included, he meant it...even if he couldn't be bothered to put it on an inventory.

The steps down to the garage and store were lit by one of those lights on a timer which, of course, turned off just as I came to the door.
After some fumbling I had it open and, across the cool garage area I quickly located the door of our store.
The key needed two turns to unlock the big heavy galvanised steel door, which opened to reveal cob-webs and dust and the gloomy interior.
Some groping about on the wall beside the door and the light switch was found. What was re-vealed would have been an eye opener, if I hadn't

got cobwebs on my face and was struggling to get them off!

Once some equilibrium was restored, I looked around the surprisingly large space. There were half inflated pool toys, a couple of very dusty chairs and there, in the corner, much to my delight, the golf clubs!
I explored them without delay.
One bag did contain a motley collection of mostly cheap clubs. However the other bag contained a complete set of PING irons and a couple of serviceable woods. Expensive purchases when new.

Although only a complete novice with a golf club, I'd hoped that my eldest son, who'd shown some aptitude for the game in his teens, and I could use this equipment in the future on the splendid golf course at the bottom of the hill.
When I told him about the clubs in the store, he immediately said, 'Well, I'd better use the PING set, Dad. We don't want you breaking them.'
Cheeky blighter!

A full set of bedding and towels came with the place (but again didn't feature on the inventory) and Bee, being Bee, got them all out and sifted through them, washing those she wanted to keep and condemning a surprisingly small amount to the bin.
The apartment came with a washing machine (which did warrant a mention in the inventory) which, after giving it a good clean, Bee declared as serviceable.

Well, it was serviceable in that it worked and performed the task of washing things well enough. But it also leaked, and danced.On the spin cycle, it seemed to pause, draw a deep breath, and proceed to pummel the floor with a deafening drumming noise as it wriggled and jiggled across the floor. If it wasn't for the wire and the hoses attaching it to the building, I'm sure it would have boogied right out of the door!

We apologised to our charming and very welcoming Spanish neighbours, Maria and Juan, for the noise, and ventured out to buy a new one.

CHAPTER 10: SPANISH TRADESMEN

The term '*electrodomesticos*' is fairly self-explanatory to the English mind so we chose to visit one on the out-of-town shopping complex nearby. We decided that, while the mighty supermarkets might be cheaper, they were unlikely to offer a fitting service, and we'd learned long ago that plumbing and I do not mix.

Slightly nervously we asked at the desk if anyone spoke English and were delighted when one of the smartly uniformed sales assistants said, 'I do, a little.'

She was fluent and knowledgeable in all the technical aspects of the various domestic appliances laid out before us.

We quickly established that yes, installation and delivery were included, as well as disposal of the old machine. Given the weight and size of a washing machine, this last point had concerned me particularly; so that was a relief.
We listened attentively as the various benefits of each machine was described but selected an LG largely because, to be honest, we recognised the name. We also chose a microwave while we were at it.

'What time tomorrow would you like the washing machine to be delivered?' the sales assistant asked.

What? Tomorrow?

Oh yes, we'd heard all about the Spanish '*mañana*' culture. We knew what 'tomorrow' meant!

But no; specific time slots were being offered, and as good as their word, the tidy uniformed fitters arrived spot on time and installed the machine, including changing the plug and testing it, without fuss the next day.

Who says the Spanish are lazy?

CHAPTER 11: NOW WE'RE COOKING

As we looked around our 'fully furnished' apartment, it quickly became clear that we would have to replace quite a few things pretty soon to make it liveable. Next up for critical attention from Bee was the filthy patio furniture and particularly the large plastic table, which had languished outside in the sun, providing target practice for generations of passing birds, by the look of it.

I turned it onto its side to examine how to remove the legs.

Clunk. One of the legs fell off.

The rest followed after a few sharp taps, and the sun-bleached remains were interred in the bins at the end of the street.

With all the fuss about which bin should be used

for which type of waste in the UK, I was a little concerned that we were putting it in the right place, but as lifting the lid revealed half a radiogram and a child's chewed chair, I decided to add the old TV to the collection without troubling my conscience too much.

Mind you, our shopping list was growing as our tidy-up efforts increased, so we began to think that 'fully furnished' was stretching it a bit. But our new washing machine played a cheery little song rather than emitting the normal 'beep' when it finished its programme, so that made us smile.

Life in Spain was looking good so far.

'Bob!' Bee called me to the bathroom one morning. 'There's a puddle on the floor by the toilet!'
'It wasn't me!' I protested.
I think I convinced her, so I rolled up my sleeves, got down on my knees and investigated further as Bee peered over my shoulder..

'I think I see what is happening here,' I pointed beneath the cistern. 'After a flush the water continues to flow into the bowl slightly. There's a small leak somewhere between the cistern and the loo itself.'

We needed a plumber.

Time to call Peter Gunn again.

'No problem,' he told me. 'Leave it to me. I'll send Denilo round. 'He's a sort of odd job man who cleans my pool,' Peter explained. 'He helps with small jobs on my house and on the properties I hold keys for on behalf of the owners.'

'How much does Denilo charge?' I asked Peter.

'It's €15 per hour, and you buy the parts.'

Bargain! No plumber in England would so much as lift the phone for that sort of hourly rate.

Sure enough, within a couple of hours, there he was.

Denilo, with a ready smile, was a personable, slim but strong looking young man, and after a short inspection announced, in quaint but pretty good English, that we needed a new 'inside'.

The best way to solve the problem, he said, was to remove the working parts of the cistern and replace them and a few seals with new.

Without delay he fixed the loo and, as he was there, we found a few other jobs for him to do, including fitting locks to the big patio doors which, it appeared, had remained unlocked for years.

He was a careful and diligent worker and was proud of what he did. So much so that when his alteration to a bolt to make it fit those patio doors didn't come out as planned and looked a little unsightly, he sighed and said, 'No good. No. I not charge you for this work. I very sorry.'
He would not be convinced to take any payment for that little job, even at €15 per hour and even though the bolt in question was hidden from view behind a curtain!

Of course the cooker didn't work either.
Or rather the hob worked but the oven and grill stubbornly refused to produce any heat.

Peter Gunn, bless him, came up with the number of an engineer who would come and have a look.

'Eees no working,' he announced, and we waited for further information.
When none was forthcoming, I attempted to ask if it could be repaired.
'Eees no get hot,' was the reply.

Although this information was not new to us, I remained calm. 'What can be done?'
'Weeel,' he stated, sucking air over his teeth in the

time-honoured style of tradesmen the world over; 'Eeef choo like I can try to seek new hotter for him.'
'OK...' So what we needed was a new 'hotter' it seemed.
Could he get us one?
'Eees no easy.'
No surprise there.
'Eees old and no work, but I try.'

We were due to return to the UK in a few days, so once again we threw ourselves on the kindness of Peter Gunn and arranged for him to hold the keys of the apartment to deal with eventualities such as this.

Little did we know that he was going to be kept busy.

Once back in England, we received regular reports to the effect that a new 'hotter' had been located, ordered, was delivered several weeks later and, with Peter's kind assistance as doorman, was installed.
The old element, or 'hotter', had been carefully wrapped in paper and left on the hob with a bill, to prove it had been done, to await our next visit.

Once again our fears about Spanish tradesmen had been dispelled. But soon it would be time to start the improvements we had planned.

CHAPTER 12: COOL IT!

Back in Spain again, I decided we'd been far too dependent on Peter and Holly to get us out of scrapes and sort out builders for us, so I decided to do some research on my own.

Gary, a cockney chap who advertised his wares in the local paper, assured us that he'd fitted air conditioning to 'loads of places' in our area and even some on our own urbanisation.

As there was no language difficulty, I asked him to provide us with a quotation to supply and fit air conditioning to the entire apartment.

'No bother, mate! Easy job!' he chirruped. 'What sort of units d'you want? You realise you'll 'ave to pay for the units up front?'

Our apartment had been designed with conduits built into the walls so that air conditioning could be tidily fitted at a later date, and we'd seen neat installations on other local houses so we expected it to be a straightforward job.

'Easy!' said Gary 'I'll run new conduits arrand the edges of yer ceilings and dump the external units on your patio, by the doors.'
'Oh no, that won't do at all!' Bee and I exclaimed in unison.
'Why don't you use the built-in conduits and put the external units on the roof?' I suggested.

'Ay?! On the roof? Nah, there's no need to do that; and them conduits will all be in the wrong places and full of cement…rubbish, these Spanish builders. Do it my way. Easy job!'

This was not going to lead to a happy outcome, I could see. 'How much will it cost?' I asked.

'Do it my way an' not a lot; but bugger about with them conduits and it'll take weeks and cost thaasands!'
'Yes, but how much?'
Gary's phone conveniently rang just then. He said he would have a think and get back to us, and went to his car to take the call.

And that was the last we ever heard from Gary.

After a pause for thought and another trip back to the UK, Bee said 'You're going to have to ask Peter, you know.'

One of the advantages of owning a place abroad is that you can leave clothes and bulky items there and travel light. In theory this lets you take advantage of spectacularly cheap airfares and avoids anxious waits by the luggage carousel.
Of course it's rarely like that in practice because budget airlines change their rules more often than their socks in what appears to be a deliberate attempt to catch out their long-suffering customers, and charge them more money for the latest thing.
So it was on this occasion for us.

Learning from the big boys, no doubt, tiny Flybe had installed some metal boxes into which we were expected to place our hand luggage. Heaven help us if it didn't fit, or if any part of it was peeking out when we slid it in.

'That will be £40, please,' grinned the check-in sadist as Bee's (Ryanair-approved) case failed to slot in.
'What!' I said 'That's almost as much as the air fare!'

The check-in girl drew on her most recent training and adopted her determined face.
'Well, its the new rules. If the bag won't fit then you can't take it on for free.'

'Just a minute,' I said. I'd had an idea.
I took Bee's bag and turned it upside down, so that the little wheels were at the top, and slid it into the nasty metal contraption. It fitted, although the wheels slightly poked out of the top because they were just a millimetre or so wider than the lip of the box.
'There,' I said. 'Its in!'
'No,' sneered our 'customer care assistant'. 'It has to all be in. None of it can stick out. £40, please.'

My argument that this new draconian rule had been bought in between our booking and arriving at check-in fell on deaf ears, and my entreaties that the bag had been used before on this very flight without issue cut no ice. Even my observation that the bag was purchased specifically to comply with the pedantic requirements of Flybe's arch rival didn't convince them.

'No! Just one minute,' said Bee and wrenched the inverted bag out of the box.

'It *will* go in!' she said and proceeded to bend the little wheels inwards by pushing them into the floor with all the strength her slight frame could muster.

Elbowing the check-in money collector aside, she levered the case into the box and pushed. To the surprise and delight of the small watching crowd in the queue, it slid in with a satisfying whoosh of air.

'There!' she said triumphantly.
'Oh, all right,' said the airline's would be top sales-person and attached the cabin label.

There really should have been a round of applause from the rest of the smiling queue, but hey, we're British, and that sort of thing isn't done!

Back in Spain we could at last address the air conditioning issue, and we had a visitor.

Kurt was all business. He turned up in smart white overalls and in a blue van bearing his company logo, exactly at the allotted time, and inspected the apartment confidently.

'Is gud here because ze builder has put in ze tubes ready,' he announced in the clipped tones that emphasised his German roots. 'Ze job vil take two men, two and vun half days, unt ze outzide boxes go in ze roof space.'

This was more like it!

'Ve recommend ze Daikin units as more modern and
bedder engineered, but I can get different if you vont, but might be ze bad move.'
He bustled about while he was talking, measuring here and there and hopping up and down from a little yellow stool he brought with him to inspect the panels where the much-discussed conduits lived.
He then squatted on his haunches, drew out a calculator and a small pad, and while mumbling to himself in his mother tongue, he made a series of unintelligible marks on the page.
'Erm, would you like a cup of coffee?' I ventured in an effort to make the conversation a little less one sided.
'No. I am finish now.' And with a flourish, he stood and raised the pad.
'Zis is ze price for da Daikin, zis for da Mitzubushi.' He pointed.

It was not cheap, but it was done with such obvious efficiency that I was impressed.

He went on to explain the specification of each unit, room by room. The biggest one in the lounge and smaller ones in the bedrooms. Each controlled by TV-style remotes and capable of acting as heaters as well as for cooling. Then he nipped down to the van for some brochures and announced, 'I go now. Here is card. You call me ven you ready und ve discuss ven work commenze.' And off he bustled.

'Well, that went well,' said Bee.

It was April 2017 when the new UK Prime Minister, Theresa May called a General Election with a view to securing herself a mandate so that she could drive through her vision of Brexit unopposed. She failed spectacularly and we were left with a hung Parliament which depended, for its ability to make any decisions about anything at all, on delicate compromises being negotiated with other parties to gain support, as well as with the factions in her own camp.
As we were to learn, Theresa May didn't do 'compromise', and her idea of negotiation was to endlessly repeat her position without taking any notice of anybody else.

Bee and I shopped carefully at the end of the following week, ensuring we had plenty of coffee, tea, soft drinks, and sugar (which took us quite a while to find as it is sold in the type of screw top Tetra Paks we associate with orange juice in the UK). If the builders were coming we needed to be ready, and experience in England had shown that the kettle was likely to be always on, preparing endless brews.

When we'd accepted Kurt's quote, he had put it in writing along with a start date which even included a start time ... 08:00 sharp. But this was Spain. If we saw anyone before lunchtime it would be a surprise.

At 08:00 precisely there was a knock at the door. We were ready because we'd seen Kurt and another man unloading equipment outside the door for a few minutes before.
So far, so punctual.

'Zis Pedro,' Kurt announced. 'Ve start now.'
'Jolly good. Would you like a cup of coffee first?' I enquired as the kettle came to the boil.
'No. Ve stop at 09:45 for five-minute break. Now ve work.'

And work they did. It was like a military operation.

Room by room Kurt laid out the materials they would require and Pedro scuttled about on the roof or on a stepladder inside. They were obviously well practiced at this because they worked in silence until Kurt looked at his watch, saw that it was 09:45 and called Pedro, who went to get something from the van.

I leaped to the kettle and offered tea or coffee.
'No. Ve have refreshment ready.' And Pedro produced a small flask.

In a flash, Kurt was looking at this watch again and without a word, they put the flask away and resumed work.

It was the same drill at lunchtime when Kurt announced they would take a twenty five minute break and with a glance at his watch, retired to the van to make some phone calls.

Pedro drew out a small canvas bag which he unrolled to reveal a *bocadillo* (baguette) and a bottle of water. He sat on the stepladder on the patio to eat it.
A little later Kurt returned and looking at his watch, admonished Pedro. It seemed time was up and the allotted 25 minutes had been exceeded.
'Ach. *Vamos*!' he snapped, and returning to the lounge where we waited helplessly, he said, 'Ach! He is Spanish. Vot you do?' And work commenced

again.

At a little before seven in the evening, they began to tidy up and put tools and materials in corners to be out of our way. With a final flourish of the dustpan and brush, at seven o'clock precisely, Kurt announced, 'Ve go now. Tomorrow ve return at eight in ze morning.' And they were gone.

We'd employed all sorts of builders on all kinds of jobs in the UK but we'd never seen anything like this pair, and the next day followed exactly the same pattern. The only hiatus in the entire operation occurred when it was time to put the extremely heavy outside units in the roof space.

Spanish properties such as ours have solid floors and ceilings and no loft hatch to the roof void. The only way to get there was up a ladder from the balcony and over the tiles. Kurt and Pedro had cut a small access way into a decorative tower which housed services and opened up into the entirely empty space under the roof tiles. The idea was that the units would be positioned in the void to protect them from the elements and as Kurt put it 'keep out of sight'.
It was a fine plan, and Kurt even agreed the design of the metal grill which would cover the opening with us as work progressed.
The hard bit would be getting the awkward and heavy external units up there.

In England, a scaffold would have to be erected in accordance with a detailed health and safety risk assessment, and winches and hoists would be employed to swing the heavy boxes over the heads of the hard-hatted operatives.

Kurt and Pedro had a step ladder.

Bee and I watched with our hearts in our mouths as Pedro balanced each of the monstrous boxes on his shoulder in turn and climbed slowly up towards Kurt who sat on the roof and said 'Yah, yah .. Come, come.' with his arms outstretched to receive the wobbling load as it was slowly passed to the top.
On the first attempt the ladder slipped a little which stopped progress but without accident. Wisely Kurt decided to lash it to a handy decorative beam to keep it steady. There was no such harness for Pedro though, and he had to teeter on the brink of disaster as before.

'Can I come up the ladder to see where you're putting the units?' I shouted up.
'Now iz not good time,' Kurt replied.
I flitted between the bottom of the ladder and the so far redundant kettle, unsure what to do for the best.
After a tense hour, the units were in position and both men, sweating profusely, came down off the roof.

The sun was hot up there, and the work was heavy and dangerous, so Kurt, in an uncharacteristic moment, declared they would take a ten-minute break, and they retired, refusing offers of water or other refreshments, to the van.

When they came back Kurt announced 'Now is good time. You come look.'

I obviously appeared nervous as Kurt explained, 'Pedro vill hold ze ladder. I vill sit on the roof and clutch your arm ven you reach me.'
'OK.' I put one foot on the ladder.

'Zis not zo easy,' Kurt said. 'You must be slow and very careful.'
Considering what they'd just been doing, this concern for my safety was only slightly reassuring.

I confess I didn't make it onto the roof, bottling out as my head reached the gutter level.
I peeped over and although I could see nothing, I announced, 'Thank you, I've seen enough.'

Kurt and Pedro were kind enough not to laugh out loud as I descended the ladder and I made sure I didn't make eye contact with them.

Bee shook her head and went to put the kettle on.

CHAPTER 13: MEET BARKLEY

Our time in Spain was limited by school holidays as well as my responsibilities towards my mother, although that became easier to manage when she moved into a care home. She wouldn't stand in our way, but she didn't like it when we were away, and even in the long school summer holiday, we felt guilty if we were abroad for much more than two weeks at a time. I was very close to my mother who was amazingly sharp and sprightly right into her late nineties but after a couple of years in the home, unfortunately she became increasingly confused and died after a short illness.

It took me a little while to sort out her affairs but when it was done, we allowed ourselves a longer break in Spain.

Now that we had functioning air conditioning and

for the time being, everything seemed to work, we decided to take advantage of the school summer holiday and come out for a longer period.

We started planning a road trip, driving down through France and this time with the dog.

Barkley is and odd concoction ... part collie, Jack Russell, and very definitely corgi, which he resembles most closely. He may be small, fluffy and sweet, but he packs a mean bark.

Having said we weren't going to have another dog after our lovely mild-mannered black Labrador dropped dead on his walk one day, Barkley charmed us on a visit to the Dogs Trust, and we adopted him.

To be fair we knew he had problems. He'd been brought over by the charity from Northern Ireland, where he'd been mistreated. The Dogs Trust wouldn't give us any details, of course, but it was clear from the time that they'd had him before even putting him up for adoption that he'd been through some nasty experiences in his short life.

We were told he had issues with barking and what seemed like aggression, although he wouldn't actually harm a fly, was house trained and knew sim-

ple commands.
His barking, which for those not in the know could seem quite intimidating even for such a small dog, was, we were told, principally an expression of fear. The poor little chap had been so badly frightened that barking became his defence mechanism, and it was going to be a hard habit to break.

We'd even hired a dog behaviourist...well, a girl who lived round the corner who was training to become one...to help us. But the barking, while it got less aggressive, persisted.

Of course we were going to take him to Spain with us. Hadn't we just bought a special seat cover that gave him a nice safe playpen in the back of Bee's VW Golf?

The route was planned to the most minute detail. We would travel to the Eurotunnel in Folkestone, Kent, and from there drive down through France over three days, staying in pre-booked cheapish hotels beside the motorways en route.

He'd be alright, wouldn't he? It was only push-bikes, cars, vans, and lorries he didn't like. Oh, and people. Of course we would enjoy the trip!

Predictably enough, that wasn't the way it worked out.

CHAPTER 14: THE ROAD TRIP FROM HELL

In the car, every time we were overtaken, slowed down, or stopped, Barkley leapt up. And if a bicycle or motorbike appeared in his line of sight, he was off, barking like crazy.
It took just long enough for us to reach the next trigger point for him to calm down.

Surprisingly he was as good as gold on the train in the Channel Tunnel, but perhaps sensing our anxiousness to find the right route as we drove off, he expressed his displeasure within yards of the terminal.

This wasn't going to be fun at all.

We reached the first overnight stop without too much difficulty, and I went to book us in while Bee took Barkley to relieve himself and see what he could find to bark at.

We'd requested a ground floor room so it would be easy to take him out without encountering too many other people, and settled him in his little folding travel kennel. He seemed OK and perhaps had tired himself out on the journey, so our thoughts turned to getting something to eat.

'D'you think we can trust him on his own if we both go to eat?' Bee asked.
'Maybe it'd be better if we ate in shifts,' I replied. 'But that's not much fun for any of us.'
'Maybe we could try that motel-style restaurant over the road to see if they'll allow us to take Barkley in,' Bee suggested. 'It looks reasonable.'
I was dispatched, French phrase book in hand, to investigate.

With a very Gallic shrug the waitress indicated that she had no objection to the dog coming in and I selected a quiet table, near one of the exits, nowhere near any other diners, and signalled to Bee to join me.

Barkley trotted into the restaurant with his nose absorbing the cooking smells and distracting him sufficiently to get to the table without causing a hullabaloo.

So far this was going really rather well.

When the waitress approached we held our breath as tightly as we held his collar. We had decided what to order and prepared a little speech to get it done as quickly as possible and, although he growled and let one short bark escape, we mostly got away with it.

Bee managed to distract him with something as the waitress bought the food, which we threw down our throats as quickly as we could.

Meanwhile more people were arriving at the restaurant, which was now starting to fill up.

Bee nipped out with Barkley while I paid the bill and, after a circuit of the car park and a brief barking session as a lorry passed by, we smuggled him back into our room.

'Well, that didn't go too badly,' I said as I rifled through the case for the Rennies.

'But tomorrow is another day.' said Bee.

We were lucky to stumble across a delightful 'services' stop by the Canal du Midi on the next day, which had a separate play park for dogs.
Bee was able to safely let him off the lead and he enjoyed dashing about chasing sparrows, and barking at them, of course.

The next nights were spent in a similar state of heightened tension until at last, after sitting in sizzling heat in a traffic jam on the motorway, we arrived exhausted in Almazara.

With some relief we introduced Barkley to the apartment, the outside area (cordoned off with reed screens in readiness on our last trip to avoid any bids for freedom), and took him for a walk through the avocado groves, where the new smells kept him happy and quiet for a while.

'This is going to be OK,' I said.
'Famous last words,' said Bee.

Bob Able

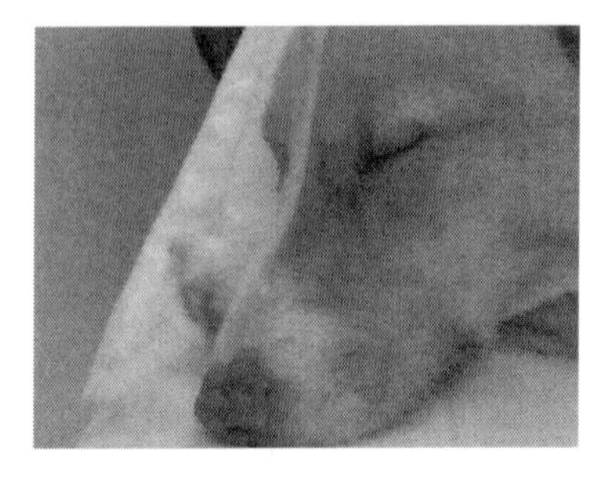

CHAPTER 15: FUN IN THE SUN

We were in Spain for a month, minus six days in total travelling. We decided to take the journey each way slowly to reduce the stress on Barkley as much as possible, but we knew people who had done it with only one overnight stop, and even one lunatic who once did it without a break; although he did say 'never again!'

Now at least we could relax and enjoy ourselves.

The pace of life in Spain is undoubtedly one of its principle attractions. Things just happen more slowly here. Unless of course you are Barkley, when every sound, sight, or smell is a whole new experience....and an excuse for a good old bark.

We took him to a restaurant with outside tables but he barked and growled at the owner who made it clear that we would be welcome, but without Barkley.

Eventually we resorted to turning the air conditioning on and leaving him in the apartment when we had to go out. At home in the UK, he usually went straight to sleep when we went out and stayed asleep until we got back, and we expected that the same would happen in Spain. But if you happen to be one of our neighbours and that ploy didn't work, please accept our apologies for Barkley's behaviour.

With his never idle tail wagging and his keen little nose enjoying the all pervading orange blossom smell, Barkley loved his walks in the avocado and orange groves on our doorstep, and one day we decided to take him to a nearby town where we had learned there was an area of beach set aside for people with dogs.

Barkley had obviously never seen a beach before and his little eyes opened wide with a mixture of curiosity and fear.

We carefully attached his extending lead and walked him down to the edge of the water.
His reaction to the sea was predictable, as he ran towards the retreating waves and away from the advancing ones, but he was obviously not afraid of the water.

Other dogs were running in and out of the waves,

and Barkley soon wanted to go and play with them, but with a busy road very close to this strip of beach, we didn't dare take his long extending lead off. That however was not going to stop Barkley.

With Bee in hot pursuit at the other end of the straining lead, Barkley hurled himself into the waves. It was very exciting, so of course he barked and barked. At least here it was OK and even expected, so we let him play until he was encrusted from head to paw in sand, salt, and seaweed.

He absolutely loved every second of his big day, except for the bath when he came home.

Driving home again after our long stay should have been the reverse of going, but there was some kind of festival in Brive-la-Galliarde in the middle

of our journey, so we couldn't stay there and had to rearrange our route.
There was nothing wrong with the town we stayed in as a result, except that the hotel had a lift, no outdoor space or nearby parking and was smack in the middle of a busy commercial area. It was a nightmare for Barkley and to get to our tiny room on the third floor was purgatory for him. As I'm not so good with stairs, the lift was the only option. Thank goodness it was only for one night.

We progressed as before along the motorways where at every toll booth, Barkley treated us to his finest vocalisations. It was the same at every roundabout, junction, and traffic light, although he was again quite content on the train through the Channel Tunnel.

As we pulled into our drive back in the UK and let Barkley out into the garden, Bee said,
'Never, *ever* again. Ever!' and went to put the kettle on.

CHAPTER 16: MEET GWEN

Glory be for the Internet! Our decision to buy a car in Spain would have been impossible without it, and identifying suitable dealers and vehicles seemed easy.

On one of our early trips over, I travelled on my own a couple of days before Bee to save a few pounds on the inevitable half-term airfare price hike, and I used the time to visit the handful of new car garages on the main road into the nearby town.

I didn't really think we could afford a new car, but initial research had thrown up that, for what they were, secondhand cars were disproportionately expensive in Spain, so I had to check.

I called into the Renault dealership first. It was a little outside the town but had the usual smart glazed showroom with gleaming examples of their latest offerings. I went in and wandered round, noticing there were no salesmen in evidence, and indeed the place seemed deserted.

I climbed into a Clío and then a Megane, and opened the doors of a couple of others, but no helpful sales person appeared.

I closed the doors smartly, thinking that the noise would bring them out. Nothing.

I walked around the back of the showroom and tried calling out. Still nobody.

So I drove away.

Next up was the Nissan dealership. Bee had a Nissan Micra once that she was very fond of, so this was to be a serious enquiry.

The showroom had several Micras with 'special offer' notices. As far as I could make out, these were pre-registered vehicles with no kilometres on the clock; a little like demonstration models in the UK.

'*¿Hablas inglés?*' I enquired timidly, trying out my appalling Spanish, as the sales girl approached.
'*¿Que?*'
I tried again.
'*No, lo siento.* (No, I'm sorry)' She replied.
I looked sheepish and helpless as I realised I hadn't prepared the next obvious question, which was to to ask if there was anybody who did speak English. A more senior man tore himself away from his game of solitaire on his computer and came over. With a sigh, he took over.
'*¿Hablas inglés?*' I tried again.
'*No.*'
Well that was clear enough, at least.

'Erm, this Micra, *cuánto es* (How much is it)?' I stumbled.
'*¿Que*?'
'How much?' I said, resorting to pointing.

He said something in machine-gun Spanish which I recognised contained numbers, but I couldn't pick them out.
'*Lo siento, más despacio repites, por favor*. (Sorry, please repeat this more slowly.)'
He looked up to the ceiling and gabbled again.

I had an idea. There was an old-fashioned calculator on one of the desks, so I picked it up and pointed to it.

'*Escribir el precio, por favor*' or as near to 'write the price, please' as I could manage.
The salesman grunted and snatched the calculator. He entered a number which was much more than I expected and may even have been more than the new car price.

I handed the calculator back to him with a shake of the head. 'Too much!' I said.

He looked disappointed, but with a shrug pointed at the car and entered a different figure which was several thousand cheaper.

This didn't make any sense at all, but the price was still way too high for us in any event, so I said, 'Thank you, but no.'

Then to my surprise, the salesman, who you may remember spoke no English at all, said 'Well, that is best price you get anywhere!'

I left it at that.

Decision made that it had to be a second-hand car, I retreated to review the options.

Before I flew out to Spain, I'd contacted one garage online who were based in a nearby village. I'd arranged to look at a Toyota Corolla at a specific time on a specific day, once Bee had arrived.

We set off to find the village in our hire car and located the garage without difficulty. I'd been emailing the garage owner, Adam, from the UK about this car for some days before I flew over and I knew he spoke, or wrote, excellent English. He had suggested the date and time of our viewing.

Bee wasn't so keen. 'Toyotas are like white goods,' she said. 'Worthy and functional but boring.' But, she agreed we should at least look at this one and make contact with the garage, who seemed to have a lot of stock and were, over the Internet at least, very helpful. Maybe something from their other stock would suit us if the Toyota was no good.

We duly arrived, on time, for our appointment and asked in the untidy office for Adam.
'He no here today,' we were informed.
We explained about our appointment to see the Toyota.

'¿*Que*?' Blank stares all round. 'No Toyota here.'

We explained again and produced copies of the

emails.
'Adam not here.'
'Well, could we see the car?'
'*No es posible. No aquí.* (It's not possible. Its not here.)'

I was getting beyond confusion and heading towards anger. 'But our appointment…'
Another individual in the office joined the conversation. 'Choo see,' he said in better English, 'Eees no our car. None are our car. We justa sell them.'
So you're offering cars for sale that you don't own?
'*Sí.*'
'And the Toyota?'
'The owner, she use the car today for work.'

I began to despair.
'Well, maybe we could see some of your other cars since we are here?' said Bee. 'Have you anything else in our price range?'
'*Sí!*' smiled the salesman, perking up; and tapping a few keys on his laptop, he turned it round so that we could see the screen.
'Great! Can we look at those then?'
'No.'
'Pardon?'
'No, choo need to make appointment.'
'Are the cars here?'
'No. Choo need to make appointment, then we call owners. We are brokers.'
We said thank you and left.

Online I'd discovered what appeared to be another quite large used car dealership with branches in several towns, who advertised in English and German and claimed they specialised in cars for the expat community. We set off to find them.

'Do you speak English?' I asked wearily as the salesman approached.

'Certainly, sir, how can I help you?'

He was as English as we were, and through his professional guidance and support, we discovered a little Ford KA with very low mileage (or rather kilometres) on the clock, which we bought. It might be tiny, but it was going to save us a lot of money when compared to all those hire cars we kept using, we reasoned.

We were excited to start exploring as we headed off into the sunset in the car we christened Gwen due to the letters GWN in her number plate. The name suited her slightly fussy 'auntie' image and reassuring smiling 'face'.

CHAPTER 17: LET'S HAVE A BARBECUE

Obviously eating and cooking outside is part of the whole sunny experience of life in a climate like that in Almazara, and being a keen, if frequently frustrated, barbecue user in the UK, I was anxious to secure the means to cook outdoors.

The supermarket in the nearby town had a section dedicated to barbecues with a wide range and all the accessories you could imagine. It even featured huge paella cookers powered by gas. I didn't think we were ready for the latter, but I hastily loaded the trolley up with a charcoal barbecue, the coals, firelighters, and a selection of tools from the vast array available.

While Bee looked at the nearby saucepans, I discovered, and added to the trolley, a gadget which looked like a hairdryer but which, when you pulled the lever repeatedly, blew air like an old-

fashioned bellows to get the coals glowing with minimum effort.
There were chrome grills which opened so that you could put fish in them, rotisseries, long-handled spatulas and forks and all kinds of innovative and probably largely useless tools for the outside cook. I was in heaven.

Bee, having selected a few glasses and a couple of bowls, looked in the trolley, sighed, and returned some of the more outlandish devices to the shelves while I examined the meat counter to decide what to cook.

We would have burgers of course, those Aberdeen Angus ones looked great, and sausages and chorizo. We would need chicken fillets to make kebabs, and beer. We needed beer, of course.
Bee selected salad items and some wine, and with a small tool kit for me, to help construct the barbecue, we were good to go.

A few days later, I was down by the store getting the charcoal out when our neighbours, Maria and Juan, drove in.
After the slightly awkward bilingual greetings, I noticed that Maria, who spoke better English, was looking at the charcoal with some concern.
'Choo buy *barbacoa*?' she asked.
'Yes, we did. We've used it a couple of times now with excellent results.'

'Where choo put *barbacoa*?' she asked.
'Erm, on the terrace,' I said. 'Why?'

'Is no gas?' Juan had joined the discussion, and I saw he was looking as concerned as Maria.
By means of a reply I pointed at the half-used sack of charcoal.

The Spanish have a distinct way of wagging their index finger, with side to side like a windscreen wiper being the preferred movement. The meaning was immediately clear. I had made some social faux pas.

'The fire, he no good.'
Maria took over the conversation as Juan was struggling. 'Is not good to use the fire, better the gas.'
She went on to explain that the Residents' Association had recently written to all the owners to ask them not to use charcoal barbecues because of the danger of escaping sparks, especially as the hot weather had left the surrounding woods and fields like tinder.

I felt awful. I really hadn't thought this through. It could have been me that started a fire and destroyed this wonderful place.
I put the charcoal straight back in the store and, as far as I know, it's still there, along with the hardly used barbecue. The hunt for a gas barbecue was on.

'*Where on earth do you buy gas*?' I thought. They didn't sell it in the supermarkets.
'And,' said Bee, 'what are we going to do with all this meat you bought in the meantime?'

So back we went to the supermarket. They could sell us a gas barbecue, certainly, but my Spanish wasn't good enough to understand the answer about where to get gas, even if it was good enough to ask the question, which, of course, it wasn't.

In the UK my best pal had bought an electric barbecue and claimed it was no bother at all.
There was a power point on the balcony. It was a thought. There was a range of electric teppanyaki grills in the supermarket. We had no idea what teppanyaki was, but they were very cheap and would do to cook for the two of us tonight, we reasoned, so we bought one.
It worked pretty well and, even if it it did take an age to heat up, at least it didn't spark.
It was too small to cook anything substantial, but as a backup it would do nicely.

'We still need to get a proper gas barbecue, though. If I could just work out how to buy the gas,' I said.

'Well, you know what to do,' said Bee. 'Ask Peter!'
So I did.

Peter told me that not far away, on an awkward junction set up from the main road near the motorway, there was a small English-run supermarket.
Assuming we couldn't find an old gas cylinder in a ditch somewhere and just pay for a refill, they could set us up with a gas 'contract', similar to the ones we have in the UK, and sell us a gas cylinder.

We found the place eventually, and it was all a bit odd, to say the least. It was part of the ground floor of a grubby detached building set on its own, right by a busy main road, but accessed from a bumpy side road. The upper floor seemed to be scruffy flatlets with washing flapping on the balconies. A large plastic sign declared that it was an English supermarket, and displayed a very faded picture of a Union Jack.

Inside there were a couple of aisles offering a handful of things that the British would recognise, such as tea bags, marmalade, toiletries, pint glasses, and a few tinned items.
Running along one wall was a glass butchery counter on which a few stale looking cooked meats languished, with a notice saying they would prepare a frozen 'meat package' containing 'everything you need for your holiday', including burgers, sausages, and ribs 'English style'.
There was also a tiny bar with a beer tap, in front of which, at one of the mismatched tables, the cor-

pulent British owner sat disconsolately nursing a cloudy pint of beer beside a hand-written notice saying 'Internet café' and an ageing laptop.

The whole place seemed very down at heel, but they did indeed sell gas cylinders, and we signed up for a contract with 'Cepsa gas' and drove away with a new full cylinder in the boot.
Within a couple of months the shop was closed down and boarded up, so perhaps we'd been lucky.

The following day we went back to the original supermarket and purchased a compact gas barbecue which would be ideal for our needs and could cook for four, or six at a pinch if the need arose, quite comfortably. My little tool kit was deployed to help assemble it, and the gas was connected up.

It worked perfectly first time and serves us well to this day, and best of all, it doesn't spark.

When we saw Peter some time later, he showed us his large paella dish and the gas cooking ring he'd bought to heat it.
'It's great for a party or a family gathering,' he said.
'No!' Said Bee. 'Three barbecues are quite enough.'
And that was the end of that idea!

CHAPTER 18: OUR FIRST VISITOR

Peter Gunn had been generous with his time and advice and particularly so when we asked him about the local shops and restaurants. He and Holly took us to an out-of-town place to introduce us to the *menú del día* system many Spanish restaurants offer, which is usually the cheapest way to enjoy a full meal.

Originally designed for farmworkers and the like who, as is the traditional Spanish way, would eat their main meal at lunchtime (taken at about two o'clock in the afternoon), the *menú del día* might offer limited choice but consisted of two, or more usually three courses with a glass of beer or wine thrown in.
Prices vary widely from €8 a head to an astronomical €25 in the pretentious hotels on the sea front who have forgotten the rustic tradition the *menú del día* was based on.

Bee and I avoided the higher priced establishments and searched for *menú del día* in the midrange.
We discovered the delights of a refreshing gazpacho, various elegantly presented tasty starters, fish dishes, meat and stews, followed by delicately pretty *'postre'* or desserts.
Generally these meals are beautifully presented and mostly well cooked, but always made with care using the freshest ingredients and served by friendly staff.

Anybody who tries to tell you that Spanish cooking is greasy and dull is absolutely wrong. That might have been true in some of the nastier tourist places in the 1960s, '70s and '80s, but modern cuisine culture in Spain, at least in our bit of it, is a match for anything in the world.
There are, for example, several restaurants with one, two, and even three Michelin stars within five miles of our apartment, and even their lesser competitors strive to produce the very best food, and take great pride in doing so. Even when it comes to that much abused and often maligned dish, paella.

We discovered a traditional paella place in the *campo*, or countryside, which specialised in this dish at lunchtime. As we ate, under a broad pergola covered in vines which gave just enough shade on a delightful sunny afternoon, with a gentle breeze cooling us as we sipped the excellent

house wine and admired the view to the mountains, above our heads, a large rat strolled unconcerned across the pergola towards the kitchen.
We drew the matter to the waiter's attention, who shrugged and said, '*Es normal.*'
The paella, however, was excellent.

Our first visitor was our eldest son, Richard.
He was due to fly out with his girlfriend then take us to the airport a couple of days later and have a week with her in Spain on his own.
The flights were all booked and paid for when the girlfriend announced that she wasn't coming and was moving out. Long discussions followed as to what to do, and in the end, we agreed that Richard would still come over on his own, but I would stay on with him after Bee, who had to work, went back to England.
He obviously needed a break and a bit of cheering up.

This meant changing the names on flights and cancelling others but we sorted it out, and our plan to try out those golf clubs in the store was still on.
I also couldn't wait to take Richard to some of the places we'd discovered, such as El Toro, which served the most magnificent, enormous, and succulent steaks, and of course, the traditional paella

place where we'd seen the rat!

But first on the agenda was to sort out a round of golf.
The prices in the pro-shop at the golf club for a round and the hire of a buggy, which was essential with my dodgy back, were mildly terrifying, so when we met Holly and Peter for a drink to introduce Richard, the subject came up.

As ever Peter had the solution.
'There's a booking agency nearby which can book green fees for you at much cheaper rates,' he told me. 'They sell discounted golf gear if you need it too.'

The next morning Richard and I set off to find it and he took the wheel for his first experience of driving on Spanish roads.
The entrance to the booking agency wasn't its most prepossessing feature, being a small doorway between a used-car showroom and one of those Chinese shops you see everywhere in Spain that sell everything from pegs to patio heaters.
When we got to the first floor, however, it was clear that the agency, which was as much golf and sports shop as booking agent, covered a large area over several shops and had most professional multi-lingual staff.
We booked our round of golf with ease at a much-reduced price and bought ourselves a pair of golf

shoes and some gloves each, yet only spent a little more than we would have done on just the green fees in the clubhouse.
In Spain sometimes it's not what you see on the outside (indeed we'd walked past the entrance to this place several times without noticing it) as much as who directs you to the right place that counts. Once again we owed thanks to Peter and Holly for putting us onto this golfer's goldmine.

The last time I'd picked up a golf club was to hack round a scruffy pitch and putt in Norwich with Richard. Now what lay before us was a beautifully manicured and reputedly quite challenging proper golf course in the sun, and it seemed to be getting hotter by the minute.

We were shown how to use the onboard GPS linked computer scoring system in the buggy, and the official asked if we would mind if another player joined us, who was on his own and just wanted some practice. So long as he understood that we were novices then fine, and as he only wanted practice rather than a game, we saw no reason why not.

We exchanged pleasantries with Steve as we walked to the first tee.
'What's your handicap?' he asked.

'Twenty-eight,' we both chimed. 'What's yours?'
'Well I'm a bit out of practice, so I'm probably only about an 8 now,' he said.
Practice indeed! We hoped he would be gentle with us.

Of course he was stunning, and we were hopeless, and I got progressively worse as we laboured on. At least he was patient with us and helped find endless badly hit balls.
Although I was extremely glad to see the cold beer in the club house at the end of the round, we did enjoy ourselves.
We also learned that there is a pay-as-you-go driving range adjacent to the course which was open to all. That, we resolved, would be the limit of our endeavours for a while.
Until we got used to those new clubs, you understand!

CHAPTER 19: OUR FIRST HAGGLE

As Bee and I toured around, getting used to the area in our little car, we came across Jalón, a village in the mountains famed for its wine and its market. This compact town is the usual mix of the picturesque and the tumbledown but has added charm with the most enormous *'rastro'* or flea market once a week.

The stalls stretch for a considerable distance along the road and offer everything from antique paintings to dubious 'designer' clothing. It's always heaving with people and crammed with competing traders close together in an orgy of bargain hunters and rogues. It's great fun if you keep your wits about you and are prepared to haggle.

My first attempt at securing a bargain was not my proudest moment, however.
I was very much in need of a hat and given the choice of four or five sellers (some next door to each other) offering broadly the same goods, I tried on a few.
It wasn't long before I found myself visiting the same stall for the second time, which piqued the stall holder's interest.
'Eeengleeesh?' he enquired. 'You like? Very good straw. From Gata de Gorgos. Made the best hands by!' I was informed when I balanced the simple beach hat on my head in front of a small faded mirror.
'How much?' I asked.
'I make good price. He suits you. Best quality and good fit too. €30.'
€30! This sort of hat is half that price in any souvenir shop by the sea, I thought. I took it off and put it down. 'No thanks,' I said.
'You not see thees quality in seaside shops,' he said 'Thees made by craftsman in Gata by hand. Will last for years!'
I did need a new hat, and it was quite well made, so I thought I'd try an offer.
'How about €15?' I suggested.
'€28' was the immediate response.
'No. I won't pay more than €20,' I said firmly.

So a few minutes later, and €25 lighter, I was the

proud owner of a new hat, and Bee and I moved on to other stalls.
'Umm, I don't know what happened there, Bee,' I said, 'But I seemed to get a bit carried away with the bartering.'
'So I see,' said Bee with a sideways look at the hat and an eye roll. 'I suppose you want a new leather belt next?'

Yes, I did, as it happened. And there was the man to help me.
As we watched he shortened belts, moved buckles, and made extra holes in the most exquisite thick leather.
'*Aquí* (here), no problem,' he announced.

I still have the magnificent belt I bought, but the hat, which if I'm honest is slightly too small, lives in a cupboard.

Most Spanish towns have wonderful produce markets, selling everything from oranges to fish and from meat to cabbages. Almazara in that respect is typical. What is exceptional however, is that Almazara's market is held indoors in a fascinating ancient high-ceilinged building, like a miniature version of the famous markets in Valencia and other big cities. Almazara's market, however, isn't aimed at tourists but is the mainstay of the shopping experience for all the indigenous population.

Very few of the stallholders speak any English and they're quite likely to use the impenetrable *Valenciano* language (which, it was pointed out to me, is *not* a dialect) as their principle means of communication.
To protect and promote this ancient language, one or two of the Town Halls, including ours, have started to produce letters and documents in *Valenciano*, but, for ours at least, unfortunately nobody has suggested that they might be wise to also put a Castilian Spanish translation in alongside it, let alone English or any other language. It causes considerable aggravation, but at least their attempts to save the language are well meant.

The entirely fresh produce in the market is fabulous in any language, and is superbly and often artistically presented as stallholders attempt to sell their wares against their competitors.
There's a separate room with massive marble slabs for the fish sellers to display their large red prawns, cuttlefish, hake, cod, spider crabs, and lobsters, along with various sea creatures I couldn't name, just yards from where they were taken from the sea.

Then there's the larger main hall where butchers will cut, trim, and prepare just what you want in front of you, as you watch.

They are adjacent to the most dazzling multi-coloured vegetable and fruit stalls, each trying to steal the show with their elaborate displays of wonderful fresh produce.

You can buy, as we did initially, by pointing and nodding and although a little daunting at first, given how busy it all gets, the market traders smile and encourage, but never push.
Interspersed with these sellers are bakers and florists, olive sellers and, surprisingly, four or five little bars offering coffee, beer, wine and spirits, and authentic tapas made on the spot in front of the foot-weary customers.
Each 'pitch' is permanent in that the traders seem to have set areas, and some have become more like shops, but each is frequented by an enthusiastic and loyal customer base.
A visit to this friendly bustling emporium is a joy, and we love it, especially now that one of the stallholders has started to recognise us and has a glass of wine and a tapa ready for us whenever we go.
We have never had the same thing twice at this stall and the owner imports all sorts of exotic pickles, salsas and tinned or bottled fish, and is very inventive with them.
We have enjoyed salt cod on a piece of bread with marmalade and chilli pickle, anchovies on bread with a drizzle of spiced olive oil, sliced cheese with a caramelised sweet pepper and port pickle,

scorpion fish pate ... the list goes on and on. When you add a glass of good quality wine and all for €3 a throw, it is easy to see why we keep going back! The market enchanted us on our first visit, and the feeling hasn't diminished however often we go.

◆ ◆ ◆

The market doesn't sell everything we might need unfortunately, and for all those other things shopping can be a bit of a trial at first, or even when you get used to it if you don't keep your wits about you. Recently confusion reigned as something else caught us out in the supermarket.

Not having long to spend shopping on this particular morning, with a pressing arrangement to meet for drinks pending, we rushed round the big supermarket and gathered up a few essentials. We'd filled our trolley with the vital things we needed, like washing powder, loo rolls, and of course wine, and headed for the checkout, down the vegetable aisle to cut off the corner.

'Hang on', said Bee brightly, bringing the trolley to a rapid stop, 'Look at that!'
We always had trouble buying spring onions of the size we were used to in our salads. The Spanish onions we'd found, although mild in flavour, were huge and just one would last us a week.

Above the usual enormous offerings, on a separate shelf, were bunches of just the right size with all the foliage still in place.
'At last,' she said as she flung a bunch into the trolley at the last moment and headed for the tills.

The following day was one we'd set aside to eat at home. With such wonderful flavoursome produce available so cheaply, we tried to take advantage of what was around us and local and make our own version of the Mediterranean diet at least twice a week.
'Just pass me those spring onions from the fridge,' said Bee. 'I'm going to make a salad.'
I should point out at this stage that Bee has suffered horribly from hay fever most of her life. It eases off in Spain but over the years, it seems to have deadened her sense of smell to some degree. So when I opened the fridge, the waft of garlic which hit me was worthy of comment.

'Coo! Have you got some huge garlic thing in here?' I said as I reeled back.
'There are a couple of garlic cloves in there, yes,' she said. 'Why?'
'Just a bit of a whiff of the stuff when I opened the fridge is all!'
'Yes well, pass me those spring onions and get out of the way,' she instructed.
'Wait a second,' I said as she chopped. 'Are you sure about these?'

'What d'you mean?' Bee growled as the first one dropped into the salad.
'Hang on,' I reached over, 'let me try that.'
Sure enough the flavour engulfed me as soon as the unfortunately quite large bite I'd taken was in my mouth.
'Gawd and Bennett! That's wild garlic!' I exploded.
When my eyes stopped watering enough, I found and examined a small label buried in amongst the leaves.
'*Ajo tierno.*' Wild garlic it was.
'Honestly,' said Bee, 'You just cannot buy proper spring onions here!'

And wasteful it may have been, but I'm afraid despite being regarded as a delicacy in Spain, the rest of that bunch went in the bin.

The one at the end of the street, that is!

CHAPTER 20: TAXING TIMES

At last it was our turn, and Lucia Teresa Martinez de Carrio (according to the sign in front of her) beckoned us to her desk and indicated that we should sit.

We'd been waiting quite a while, and the hard wooden visitors' seats under the window onto the street, currently in full sun, were getting hot.
The ineffectual air conditioning in the SUMA office, where we'd come to find out what the letter they'd sent us was all about, was no doubt more efficient behind the glass screen where the staff sat; however the customers, of which there were several, sweltered in the heat.

SUMA is the organisation charged with collecting various types of taxes on the Costa Blanca, and the directions to their local office amongst the shops in the nearby town were easy to follow. The reason we needed to visit however was harder to understand.

Our unlabelled letterbox is in a bank of '*buzon* boxes' at the end of the street, and this collection of lockable post boxes had been a mystery to us until we asked our solicitor to find out which little slot was ours. When he eventually got a reply from the previous owners, we had fun counting the boxes to establish which one was number 43 (a number that bore no relation to our address, by the way).
The situation was made all the more confusing when you remember that there are 30 properties in our little cul-de-sac, but for some reason there are 50 *buzon* boxes in the bank.

Needless to say there was no key for it amongst the pile left in the apartment by the departing previous owner, and according to our solicitor, they said they'd never used it so had no recollection of any keys. Once we finally established which little locked flap was definitely ours, and that we were within our rights to force it open if we had to, I set to work.

Most of the boxes were stuffed full of junk mail so it was difficult to see if ours contained anything of value from the outside.
I'd gathered up all the lost and homeless filing cabinet-sized keys I could find in our UK home

and was amazed to count a dozen of them hiding in drawers and cupboards, all with their original purpose long forgotten.

My idea was to try all these keys in the hope that one might fit and avoid the potential for me to break the little plastic flap when I forced the lock. None of them were remotely close to fitting in this little lock, so I borrowed a rechargeable drill and very carefully drilled the lock out. It was uncomfortable work as the *buzon* box is set on a very steep road leading up the mountain, where having one leg considerably shorter than the other would have been a distinct advantage.

What awaited within was a surprise. Beneath several years' worth of slightly damp junk mail there was a layer of what looked at first like brown seeds. It took some sweeping in the confined space to get it all out, and we decided it was probably several generations of insect nests, although what had made a home there we never discovered.

In amongst this mess we found two letters, both bearing SUMA franks; one a final demand addressed to the previous owners and dated five years previously, and near the top a letter addressed to us.

I fought with my conscience a little before opening the letter addressed to the previous owner but, given its antiquity, I couldn't imagine that it was of any great relevance today, so I opened it. When I saw what it was, I dropped it off to our solicitor's office a few days later with a request to pass it on.

Our lawyer was somewhat amused by my honesty and suggested that, as he'd made absolutely sure there were no outstanding debts, or rather that those which were unpaid were dealt with, before we bought the apartment, we should simply chuck the letter away.

The other letter which was addressed to us was more of a mystery. It was in Spanish and seemed to be demanding an overdue payment. The letter had been sitting in the box for some months before we discovered it, and Peter and Holly could make nothing of it when we showed it to them. They suggested we should visit the SUMA office to sort it out and also explained that we could arrange to pay all our taxes by direct debit there, so nothing would get missed the future.

So now, as we took our seats in front of Lucia Teresa Martinez de Carrio, clutching the letter, I opened with the now familiar, '¿Er, *hablas inglés*?' Inevitably the answer was, '*Lo siento, no.*' Sorry, no.

After some pointing and head scratching and, on reading the letter with a nod and some furious keyboard bashing on her computer, Lucia was joined by a colleague from the back room who, we were relieved to find, spoke some English.

She introduced herself by doing that distinctive 'windscreen wiper' style finger wag and tutting.

'Choo not pay. Choo must pay in January,' she informed us.

'Well, OK, but what is this for?'

'Ees choo tax for *coche*...car. Choo car,' and she pointed to some numbers and letters which, with a start, I recognised. They ended in GWN. Of course! This was Gwen's car tax bill!

But hang on, we didn't buy Gwen until October, so surely we only owned the tax from then?

It seemed not. The previous owner, and the garage we bought it from, had obviously omitted to pay the tax, and when the registration passed to us, the SUMA office had caught up and now wanted to charge us for the whole of the previous year.

I tried to explain that we didn't own the car for all of the period in question, but our English speaking SUMA lady, whose name I hadn't been told, explained that we were still liable to pay the whole bill because the previous owner hadn't done it.

I was becoming quite cross about this injustice but Bee, who'd been studying the bill while I discussed it, dug me in the ribs to get my attention and was tapping her finger on the paperwork.

'Just pay the nice lady, and then we can get on and

put all this stuff on direct debit,' she said.

I looked at what she was tapping. The bill for the whole year was less than twenty euros. So with a smile, I asked if they would accept cash and paid up. Car tax is cheap in Spain, it seems.

The business of getting the rest of our tax payments made by direct debit was much less straightforward however.

It seemed Lucia's job was to deal with each enquiry initially and, if she couldn't resolve it on the spot, to pass the customer on to someone else or, more likely, send them away with instructions to make an appointment to see the right person.
The queue behind us was growing considerably, and I was aware of some pointed shoe tapping and sighing behind me.
Given the limited hours the SUMA office was open and the time we'd been there already, the queuing customers' frustration was understandable.

'*No es posible*,' Lucia said when I asked about my taxes. 'Your house papers you must bring me,' the nameless English-speaking lady added. 'Fix day with Lucia.'

Fixing a day with Lucia was easier said than done, but with some pointing at the calendar on her desk and a considerable amount of keypad bashing, at last an appointment was made for us to return to the office, with our house deeds, in a few days' time.

Having been warned that Spanish officialdom is often a longwinded paper chase, we gathered up everything we could think of that might come in handy for our meeting with the nameless English speaking SUMA representative.

Into a large envelope we stuffed the house deeds, some letters from our lawyers, two bank statements, and a letter in English from our Spanish bank manager. We added our plane tickets and the bill from the guy who mended the cooker for good measure. As we already had our driving licences and bank cards in our wallets, we were sure we had all the bases covered.

'*Pasaporte y NIE,*' said Lucia as we reached the head of the queue.

It took a while, but we got her to agree that we could drop our passports and NIE numbers in later, and she allowed us to move to the next desk, where the nice, but still nameless, English-speaking lady offered us a seat.

She examined the house deeds and the bank statements but barely glanced at the other information and set it aside. Much to my surprise, she then turned the computer screen towards us to reveal a plan showing our urbanisation and asked us to

point at which property was ours.
That done, she zoomed in and wrote down a series of numbers which were now legible and checked them against the deeds. More key tapping ensued until, seemingly satisfied, she printed off several pages of unintelligible Spanish which she proceeded to lay out in front of us.
As we were not residents, she informed us, it would be possible for us to access our tax affairs, in English, from the UK if we downloaded a piece of software onto our computer.
One of the pieces of paper contained a website address and an enormously long sequence of letters and numbers, which she said was our initial log-on details which we must keep safe at all costs. The software, she said, would walk us through the registration process in English and, when we returned with our passports and NIE numbers, she would issue us with a password for use when we first logged on.

Next we had to visit another adjacent desk, carrying some of the pieces of paper she printed off. The occupant, a mousy woman with a perm that looked as if it could resist the blast from a jet engine, indicated where we should sign them.
She proceeded to select two rubber stamps from a drawer and, having inked them, stamped both pages and directed us to take them back to the first desk.

To put this into context, this second desk was set at an angle and almost touching the first desk; it was debatable whether the occupants of these desks even needed to stand up to pass papers to each other. However we were now expected to return the stamped pages to the first desk, but, as another customer was now sitting in front of it, we were sent back to the reception area once again to wait.

'I'll nip home and get the passports and NIEs while we wait,' I said.
'There isn't time,' said Bee. 'The office closes in ten minutes!'

As Lucia rebuffed the angry approaches of those still in the queue with a wave of her hand and began to tidy her desk ready to close the office, the nameless lady finished with her customer and called us forward, much to the muttered annoyance of those waiting.

'Give papers me.' She pointed at the stamped pages we were holding. 'And *mañana* the *pasaporte* bring, no?'
'No problem,' I said.
And we were standing on the doorstep as they opened in the morning.

'*Momento*,' said Lucia as she unlocked the door and indicated that we should take up position on the

visitors' seats, which rapidly filled with the rest of the people who were waiting behind us outside.
We were definitely first in the queue however, and when she eventually called us forward and I attempted to explain that all she had to do was enter our passport and NIE numbers on our file, she said, 'Choo have appointment?'

Just as I reached boiling point, the nice but still nameless English-speaking lady looked up from her desk and, smiling, beckoned us through to her desk.
Lucia, rather flustered by this breach of protocol, looked sharply at the protesting queue members and quelled them once again with a raised hand.
Nameless wished us good morning, took our passports and NIE numbers and opened the file on her computer.
Five minutes later we were done and, with black looks from the queuing customers, we were on our way home.

Back in the UK subsequently, I loaded the software on my Mac and naturally it refused to work.
It did however put a 'certificate' on my email account, which I've had all sorts of trouble with. Being in Spanish, it causes my emails to be rejected by some recipients.
No matter what I try, I haven't been able to remove this certificate, which reappears each time

I think I've got rid of it, whenever I next use the computer.

I may be restricted to sending emails from my iPad these days, but at least all our Spanish taxes are smoothly extracted from our bank account now, with no input from me.

CHAPTER 21: LOCKED UP!

Security, or the lack of it, had always bothered me in the UK, and in Spain I became paranoid. What if we were burgled? Suppose the place caught fire? What if there was a break in? What would we do?

The arrival of the annual buildings and contents insurance renewal papers for our house in the UK heightened my concerns. The questions about type of locks and burglar alarms nagged at me. Two thousand miles away, our lovely piece of paradise sat all alone with basic locks and flammable woodland all around.
Granted, the level of crime in our urbanisation, with its 24-hour security guards regularly patrolling in their cars, was laughably low.

In the last year, just one 'crime' was reported, and that turned out to involve an over-eager neighbour accidentally breaking a car window when trying to assist a resident who'd locked her keys in her car. This would have gone entirely unnoticed if not for the fact that another neighbour happened to observe the action from her living room window opposite and, misunderstanding the situation, called the emergency services.

But no amount of warm words from Bee could calm me down. I *had* to improve the security of our apartment and ensure that there were sufficient fire precautions.

I understand this state of mind is not uncommon in owners of property abroad as they fret about how safe their investment is. Knowing it was a common thing didn't make it go away.
My first action in this daft endeavour was to seek out and purchase a fire extinguisher. Not as easy as you may think in a little town like Almazara.

Back home I had a car-type fire extinguisher in the kitchen, but search as I might, no such compact solution seemed to be available.
In the end I purchased an ungainly and heavy full-sized fire extinguisher from a builders merchants and proudly positioned it, with a matching fire blanket, in the utility room.

Coincidentally, within a matter of weeks, the Residents' Association purchased and installed similar fire extinguishers for each hallway of the

development. The nearest one to us was directly outside our front door.
I felt slightly silly but at least a bit safer from fire.

Fire protection was one thing, but what about the potential for a break-in?

I'd noticed that several of the magnificent villas nearby had wrought iron grills on the windows and doors and, now that I thought about it, these clearly weren't just for decoration. They were lockable and added another layer of security.
I needed a similar steel gate on my front door, I decided.

Denilo, after explaining that I already had a double-locking steel-faced front door, agreed that it would be possible to mount a key-locking security gate outside the front door and explained that he knew a 'metal man' who could make it for me.

Setting aside visions of a vast robot bristling with anvils and hammers, I encouraged Denilo to introduce me to this marvellous man of steel.

Santiago Manolo Sánchez was tiny.
My visions of the archetypal muscle-bound blacksmith evaporated as he rested his clipboard on the stairs and pulled a tape measure from his pocket.
But this miniature man had hidden depths. Granted we had to lend him a stool to reach up to

the top of the door frame to measure it, but despite speaking no English whatsoever, with Denilo as interpreter, he took a brief, stayed five minutes, nodded to us both, and left.

The following morning he arrived with a beautifully detailed engineering drawing of the gate, exactly as I'd envisaged it, with a fully worked-up estimate setting out materials required, sizes of steel to be used, and offering a choice of two finishes and three locking mechanisms.
To say I was impressed was an understatement, and I was more than delighted when I looked at the price.

Your average UPVC door in the UK would have been twice the price, half as secure and probably unlikely to repel so much as a determined cat. What Señor Sanchez was proposing would have impressed the Bank of England, but with an element of functional artistry that wouldn't have offended a fussy interior designer.
Without delay I commissioned the work and, given the price, chose the highest specification for finish and decoration from the options offered.

'When will it be done?' I asked Denilo, who shrugged and offered no further comment.

Needless to say we were back in the UK when, several months later, we were informed, by Peter Gunn who was keeping an eye on the works, that

the gate was finished.
With a trip planned a few weeks hence, I looked forward eagerly to seeing the completed job, and I wasn't disappointed.
It was splendid and, to my surprise, the robust business-like gate itself was softened with the use of a delicately sculptured handle with a leaf motif and a petal-shaped latch so that everything the user touched had style and finesse.

All handmade and for less than the price of a B&Q back door!

CHAPTER 22: WHAT'S THAT SMELL?

Before we bought the Ford KA, a series of hire cars had ferried us here and there, including the ubiquitous and tiny Fiat 500. This little car was omnipresent on the Spanish roads, particularly around the airports, where hire companies obviously chose them for their fleets.
A pastiche of the original Fiat 500 of the 1960s it may be, but at least it has some creature comforts such as the all-important air conditioning and, surprisingly, a goodish amount of space.
Almost unbelievably a folding table and four non-collapsing garden chairs fitted in the last one we hired, and we even got the tailgate shut!

Our long shopping list led us to discover a garden

furniture outlet nearby, and we amazed ourselves by avoiding delivery charges and cramming all our purchases into this remarkable little car.
The Ford KA was built as a joint effort with Fiat, and they shared the same floor pan and engine, so we had high hopes that the Ford KA we bought would serve us well.

But it didn't.

Our car was second-hand so we expected it to have the odd sign of wear, but with very low mileage (or should that be kilometrage) on the clock and only a few scratches, it promised much.
Whether it had been 'clocked' or not we will never know, but despite sharing the same engine as those Fiat 500s, it lacked 'get up and go' and, given that our property was half way up a mountain, we needed the same willingness those little Fiats showed to be much in evidence.

The problem was highlighted when, on one balmy evening about a year after we bought it, we decided to drive to the very top of 'our' mountain and take a nosy at the spectacular villas up there and the view that we all shared.

There wasn't even half a tank of fuel in Gwen, so she couldn't complain about extra weight, but complain she most certainly did.
Considering we'd had her serviced just a few weeks before, including a new cambelt (the ex-

pensive rubber band that all modern cars seem to be cursed with, and which, if it breaks, causes terminal engine failure), there should have been no problem.

We had struggled past some beautiful houses when Bee asked 'What's up there?' as she spotted a steep lane we hadn't noticed before.
I ground the gears as the road got steeper and, as we rounded a bend, a stench of burning clutch filled the air.
Gwen started to lose the ability to make forward progress and slowly came to a stop.

Now we were in a pickle.

Gwen smoked a bit as I used the kerb on a drive behind us to stop us rolling back helter-skelter down the hill, but other than smelling bad and coughing a bit, she continued to run, albeit uncomfortably.

Up came the bonnet, for what good that did. There was nothing there I recognised, just plastic panels and rather hot bits of metal. Nothing I, being more familiar with old Land Rovers and having never progressed mechanically beyond the Morris Minor, could identify.
'Let's let her cool down a bit,' I offered. 'If she boils I'll know what to do, but I confess this is a bit beyond me.'

'At least the walk home is all downhill,' said Bee.

Very helpful.

In the driveway behind us, next to the obligatory Range Rover, a Fiat 500 looked smugly on.
Next time we came, we resolved, we had to buy a more suitable car.

Gwen had to go. It was no good. A few days before, we'd taken Peter Gunn out to lunch and, having banged his knee as he wound his six foot-plus frame into the car, he exclaimed
'Blimey! I didn't know they made cars this small any more.' He was right; it was too small for the job. The writing was on the wall.

To be honest, neither of us had really been happy with a manual gearbox (stick shift) and driving on the 'wrong side' of the road had caused many a chortle as once again the door handle was employed to change gear.
There was nothing for it. On our next trip Gwen definitely had to go.

There is a little convenience store on the mountain where fresh-baked bread and croissants are available every morning. It's close to a restaurant/

bar which has a large terrace with views through the pine woods to the sea and the tennis club and stables next door. It's a lovely spot for a quiet drink, a coffee, or a more substantial meal, and the family that run it are very friendly.
Restaurante Relajarse is always popular with those requiring coffee or cold drinks after a work-out at the tennis club in the morning, and with residents and visitors to the mountain for lunch and evening meals.

Miguel, who speaks at least four languages fluently, his charming wife, Gabriela, and her father, Mario, share the front-of-house duties, while Mario's wife, Betina, runs the kitchen.
They employ a couple of staff at busy times and try their hardest to keep everyone in the community happy by staging events, hosting parties, and even providing a takeaway service for those that require it.

They work very hard for their money, and since we first visited the mountain house hunting, they've always made us feel at home.
Gabriela has an astonishing memory and always asks after our sons by name when greeting us each time we turn up, even after we've had a long stay in England. Miguel always finds us a table, even if they're all reserved, and it's lovely to be made to feel so welcome.
Gabriela and Miguel rent a house close to our

apartment so we also see them out and about regularly outside the work setting, as they walk past with their delightful young children, or give us wave as we drive past in the car.

They emailed us in England on one occasion to say that they were hosting a charity night in the restaurant and offering to reserve tickets. We were due to be there when the event took place so accepted the offer, and Miguel said he would put the tickets behind the bar for me.
When we called in a few days before the event for a drink, he drew me to one side and said,
'I think this should be a good night, but I don't want you to think I had anything to do with the band. The organisers booked them, so if they're not good, please, I am very sorry.'

We'd noticed before that the Spanish are often most concerned that their guests are having a good time and are comfortable, and they will go the extra mile to ensure everyone enjoys themselves, but this was a new approach!

We started to worry about what the evening would be like, especially as it obviously meant so much to them.
'Are you providing the buffet supper?' I asked.
'Yes, we will be doing that.'
'Well then, I'm sure everything will be fine, and we are bound to have fun.'

My attempts at reassurance were caught by Gabriela who was passing by with some glasses.

'I hope so,' she said. 'We working really hard to make this good. Eees important for us, and many peoples coming.'

The event, of course, was a roaring success. The food was delicious and plentiful, and the band, who played selections from the 60s, 70's and 80's were fine.
There was an unexpected moment of Spanish spontaneity which really made it for me. When the band took a break while we were eating, a thin grey-haired man who was one of the guests picked up an electric guitar (presumably with the band's permission) and played the most astonishing riffs. It wasn't long before the band, obviously impressed, abandoned their suppers to jam with him.

His playing was flawless, and he obviously had a long history with the instrument as he didn't even glance at it when he played. He soon had the place jumping and everyone dancing, and even did a couple of requests.
When he finished, to a rousing standing ovation, he simply smiled and went back to his table and supper with his family.
I have no idea who he was, but he must have been much in demand in the music business in an earl-

ier time. Perhaps he was a retired rock star from one of the 'millionaires mansions'.
He slipped away before I could find out any more about him, and although I thought I saw him playing tennis at the club next door a few days later, I never did find out who he was.

The smile on Gabriela's face next time I saw her told me that she thought the event had gone well too, and I was pleased for them that their efforts were rewarded.
I hope they repeat it every year.

◆ ◆ ◆

CHAPTER 23: FIRE!

We shouldn't forget all the fabulous lazy days of doing just what we came here for.

Bee and I aren't beach people (daft then, that we'd bought a property within sight of nearly twenty miles of the best beaches in Spain), but we are more than happy to enjoy the Mediterranean sun whenever it shines.

Up on 'millionaires mountain', as the locals call it, there was always a delightful breeze. This means that while the holidaymakers down on the beach fry in the stifling heat, we sit on our balcony, with a choice of shade or sun in a gentle breeze which alters slightly according to the tides.

Mind you, in the colder weather, or when we can look down from our vantage point over the tops of the buildings in the town and watch a thunderstorm or a rain shower heading our way, the wind blows harder here than lower down.

Our elevated position also enables us to see fires developing in the woods or the parched fields below us, before we can even smell the smoke.

In this part of Spain, fire strikes fear into the hearts of people like nothing else.
Each year hundreds of hectares of forest and precious natural heath are destroyed by raging fires, and sometimes they consume settlements or urbanisations like ours before they're bought under control.

The truly scary thing about this, however, is that a proportion of these fires are lit deliberately.
What would motivate anyone to do such a thing and destroy such wonderful natural countryside (and the local huge National Park and Nature Reserve which seems to be continually caught up in it), I simply cannot imagine.

Like all local residents, I scan the horizon with a growing sense of doom each time we hear the engines of the little spotter planes nearby, or worse still see the helicopters with their enormous canvas 'buckets' collecting water from the sea, the golf course, or even swimming pools to dump on an outbreak of fire locally.

Perhaps the worst outbreak in recent history, cer-

tainly since we've owned our property, took place in 2016 on the other side of the Montgo mountain range and a little way along the coast in Jávea and the adjacent areas. It made the national news in the UK as well as Spain and burned for days, destroying dozens of homes, hectares of forest, and ruining countless holidays.
Mercifully the loss of human life was minimal, but the devastation wreaked on the flora and fauna was truly awful.

Fortunately we'd gone back to the UK a few days before this cataclysmic event, but friends told us they could smell the smoke and were sweeping up ash for days, even as far away as Almazara.

On our next visit, the first thing I did was check my fire extinguisher and buy a smoke alarm. I'm not sure what good they would do, but they gave me at least a bit of peace of mind.

On a whim, we took a drive over to the scene of the fire a few weeks later.
Although the clean-up operation was strongly underway by that stage, there were still burned-out cars, scorched empty shells of houses, and grey ash everywhere. The catastrophic scene stretched some distance in every direction.

We felt desperately sorry for all those affected but were shocked to notice how the fire had behaved. For example, in a residential road of small detached villas, three in a row were charred shells, then one stood seemingly untouched, still with sooty but living trees in the garden. This was followed by two more burned-out shells and one burned almost to the ground.

The clean-up operation was clearly going to take a very long time, and we thanked our lucky stars that this time it wasn't us.

The media suggested that there were in fact three fires, and that at least two were started deliberately. Once again we could only wonder what would motivate anyone to do such a thing.

When we got back to the apartment, I checked the battery in the smoke alarm yet again.
It was pointless, of course, but it was all I could think to do.

CHAPTER 24: MEET ALVARO

We kept putting off entering the bazaar again for another car. Acquiring Gwen had been such a hassle with, ultimately, such a disappointing result, that we didn't relish the prospect.

But this time, at least on the face of it, we got lucky.

Bee and I decided we needed to buy something with an automatic gearbox and a more powerful engine to cope with the mountain roads, and preferably a bit newer. That was the easy bit. The potentially difficult bit was that we needed to trade in Gwen as we couldn't face the paperwork and pratfalls of selling privately, about which I'd heard such horror stories.

There was just one car showroom I had not visited before on the outskirts of the nearby town.

I knew it was there but had dismissed it as all the cars for sale appeared to be new with 'prices from' notices in the window which were not even remotely in our price bracket.
But as we were passing one day and visiting the supermarket next door, we decided to call in.

The garage was a Ford main dealership with sprawling premises and a large, mercifully air-conditioned showroom, and after a quick walk past the cars facing the road to see what they had, we went inside.

Alvaro was tall for a Spaniard, with greased black hair and pointed shoes. He was talking on two phones; a mobile and a desk phone. We approached with the meet-and-greet girl who said we should sit at his desk and wait.

As he finished his apparently quite heated dual conversations, he hung up the phones, turned on a wide and slightly intimidating smile, and said '¿*Si*?'

'Umm, do you speak English?' I enquired with a growing sense of déja-vu.

'Chess, of course,' he replied. 'How I help choo?'
'We are looking for a car,' I said, stating the obvious, 'to use when we are in Spain.'

'Choo have *residencia*?' he asked, the smile dim-

ming slightly.
'Er, no. But we own a property here and have NIE numbers.'
'Eees good,' he said, brightening again. 'How much you spend?'

Now the money was one thing, but the burning question for us was that we needed an automatic and had to be sure that we could trade in Gwen.

I came over all man of the world.
'That depends if you have anything that meets our specifications.'
I probably should have added that it had to fit our meagre budget as well, but that bit could wait.

'¿*Si*?' said Alvaro expectantly, as the meet-and-greet girl arrived at my elbow and asked if we wanted coffee.
Alvaro looked crossly at her as we declined politely, and I took the initiative.

'We need an automatic, you see, with a powerful enough engine to cope with mountain roads.'
Alvaro's eyes flicked to the gleaming new five-litre Mustang in the showroom.
'And used, not new. And we have to trade in our old Ford KA.'

Alvaro visibly shrank before our eyes. If all we had to trade was an old Ford KA, we were hardly likely to be the sort of people who could afford his new powerful Mustang.

'*Automático* is rare, choo know, in *España*. We no have many like that used. Why you no buy new? We do the finance?'
Well, full marks for trying, I suppose.
'No, we can't afford new. We want a used car. What d'you have in stock?'

Alvaro pressed a few buttons on his computer and turned the screen slightly so that I couldn't entirely comfortably see all of the stock list he was looking at. Inevitably it started from the most expensive and went down, rather than the other way round.
'How much you wanna spend?'

I'd done this little dance many times when changing cars in the UK and thought I knew how to play this one.
'Well,' I said with more confidence than I felt, 'it's all about the cost to change. It depends on what you'll give us for our car, then we'll add €2,000 to €3,000 to that.'

Alvaro would never make a good poker player and he looked crestfallen again. Obviously these paltry sums weren't going to help much towards his sales targets, so he tried to play me at my own game.
'What you want for your car?'
'No idea. Have a look at it and make me an offer. I

have all the paperwork here, and it's just outside.'

Alvaro's eyes flicked to the car park and alighted on an almost new KA that another customer had arrived in seconds earlier. He brightened again.
'No, not that one, the blue one.'
'Oh,' said Alvaro, snatching the offered file of paperwork.

After a few moments and a cursory walk round Gwen, he said, 'Sorry but I no think we have anything. Maybe a bit more budget?'
'Well,' I said, 'what's my car worth then? Let's start from there.'
'I get mechanic,' he said and walked away.

Wondering what to do next, Bee and I went back inside and sat at Alvaro's desk. We could see him talking animatedly to someone in the workshops behind a glass screen. He soon returned and asked for the keys.

'Now you must wait,' he said as the meet-and-greet girl pressed coffee, a cold drink, or Coca-Cola on us, and we watched as the mechanic roared off down the road in poor little Gwen.
It was quite a long wait, and Alvaro served two other customers, including one irate German, as we sat fending off the meet-and-greet girl's efforts to rehydrate us.
Eventually, after another heated debate in the workshop and much thumbing through the file,

Alvaro returned.

Now it so happened that I'd learned, from Peter Gunn (who else), that Spain was currently running one of those 'scrappage' schemes designed to get older cars off the road and boost the sales of more economical models. On looking into it, I'd discovered that in some instances this scheme applied to new as well as nearly new cars up to three years old. The Government would subsidise the purchase of the old vehicle up to €3,000.
I expected, given what I'd seen on various forecourts and in the papers, that Gwen was worth about €3,500 to €4,000, so it didn't seem to me that this scheme was terribly relevant to us.
However, here came Alvaro with the keys and the paperwork.
'€2,000,' he spat.

Fortunately, while shocked by this news, I kept my wits about me.
'What!' I exclaimed. 'That's less than the scrappage scheme price! You'll have to do much better than that!'
'I don' thing we have any cars choo can afford,' Alvaro said, and this time he turned the screen round sufficiently for me to read the stock list on the computer.
'No have *automáticos*,' he said, highlighting the column that showed the gearbox type 'less than €10,000 minimum.'

He grunted as if this was a physical effort, and I noticed beads of perspiration next to the sculpted greased hair line.
'No it doesn't work like that,' I said. 'What about the scrappage scheme?'
'*¿Qué?*'
'If you sell me a car less than three years old, you can give me €3,000 for my car.'
'But I only give €2,000.' Alvaro wasn't happy. I'd laid a good card.
'But we no got three years cars *automáticos*.'
That seemed to be that, and he looked pensive.
'*¡Momento!*' he exclaimed, pushing his chair from the desk as he sprinted into the back office. '¡I got idea!'

CHAPTER 25: HAGGLING AGAIN

Gentle reader, I don't know if you regularly frequent car showrooms but now, as we found ourselves abandoned in one in Spain, we started to notice the differences in our surroundings to those we had encountered in England.

Of course there were the huge plate-glass windows, potted palms, and gleaming new models to look at, but here there were hardly any people working.

Customers, of which there were a few in a queue, outnumbered staff by several times. There was a harassed-looking receptionist and a young girl sitting beside her who was obviously a trainee, the desk occupied a few moments before by Alvaro, the only salesman in sight, and a counter occupied intermittently by the meet-and-greet girl who smiled for so long and so hard her face must have been agony at the end of the working day. Her job was to appease waiting customers, some of whom were obviously less than happy, with regular offers of refreshments. She was with us again now.

'¡*Hola*!' she beamed. 'You like drink?'
'No, thank you.'
'Water?' She was not to be put off.
'Coffee or Coca-Cola?'
'Not just at the moment, thank you.'

She gasped slightly. This customer had said '*not just at the moment*'. That meant if she came back in a little while, she might succeed in her mission to press refreshment on us!
If it were possible, her smile got even wider, and she went away happy.
She had a definite maybe!

Now here came Alvaro, looking confident and more relaxed.

'What you like Fiesta auto?'
'Pardon?'
'Is no for sale thees time yet, but we have Fiesta auto I drive.'

He fished in his pocket and brought out a bunch of keys, one of which was a car key with a tag on it showing a stock number and registration.

'Come! I show!'
Alvaro was moving out of the door before I could question him further and, when we caught up with him, he was standing by a white Ford Fiesta which was around the corner in parking bays, not part of the display on the main road. With a flourish he unlocked the doors.

There were bags of shopping on the back seat and a pair of shoes in the front footwell.
'*Momento*,' Alvaro said, opening the boot and piling the shopping in. 'Thees the car I use for now before we sell. He not ready but I use.'
He plucked the shoes from the floor and threw them into the boot on top of the shopping.
'*Lo siento*, car not cleaned for sale.'
We were bemused.

'Get in, get in! We go for test,' piped Alvaro, holding the doors open.
This car was indeed automatic and though grubby, didn't look that old. The specification, judging by the slightly dusty seats, was fairly basic, but it had climate control and an over-complicated looking radio which Alvaro said worked with the telephone.
Alvaro chattered on about the car and, after a short while, once we were on quiet roads, he stopped and said, 'Now you drive.'

So I did, onto gravelly potholed lanes.

'How much is this car, Alvaro?' I asked, and, as if by divine intervention and with perfect timing Alvaro's phone rang through the car's speakers.

He seemed delighted. 'Choo see? Eees Bluetooth!' And with that he answered the call hands-free and gabbled away in Spanish at full volume.

While he was distracted, I turned up a steep hill and gave the accelerator a determined prod. I doubted if we could afford this car, but I might as well find out how it would cope with mountain roads. I caught Bee's eye in the mirror, and her glance seemed to say,'Yes dear, very nice, but we can't afford this one!'

As we pulled into the forecourt Alvaro's conversation came to an end, and without apology, he leapt out and said, 'Choo like? He is good, no?'

'How much is it?' I asked again.
'Choo pay me €6,750.'
'What, this car is €6,750?' That couldn't be right.
'No, is €8,750 minus you car for €2,000.'
Now I understood.
'But,' I said as we trailed after Alvaro back into the showroom, 'I told you I wouldn't take €2,000 for my car. It's too little.'
Alvaro sat down at his desk and looked dejected.
'But is three-year car and is *automatico*!'

As the meet-and-greet girl hitched up her smile

and made her way towards us, I told him, 'If that car is three years old, you can give us €3,000 for our car under the scrappage scheme.'
Once again the girl went through her speech and received the customary polite refusal. Alvaro stayed silent and if anything looked a little bemused. I noticed that the perspiration was back on his hair line.

'Choo like this car?'
'Yes, but we can't afford it.'
'What about €6,500 for cost to change?'
I started gathering up our keys and the paperwork. 'I'm sorry, it's out of the question.'

For some time Bee had been looking daggers at me. She hated being present at negotiations like these, especially if they dragged on. I thought that at any moment she might accept the meet-and-greet girl's offer of water and throw it at me if we didn't conclude this shortly.

'Choo no need worry, we clean and do service,' Alvaro was saying.
'I'm sorry, at €6,500 cost to change, it's too expensive for us. Thank you for showing us, but we have to go now,' and I started to get up.

Alvaro looked mortified, then with a groan, he slapped the desk hard with the palm of his hand and said, 'Alright! I give you €3,000 for you car!'

I looked at Bee.
Bee looked at me.
I looked at Bee again.

You would think that after over 30 years of marriage, I would know what she looked like, but these looks contained a sort of unspoken conversation.
'Well,' I telepathed, 'If he will give us €3,000, that means we only pay €5,500 for a three year old car.'

'True,' she beamed back. 'But it's more than we wanted to pay.'

'Ah, but it's a good car and a simple deal,' I broadcast.
'Oh, go on then!' she lasered back through gimlet eyes.

'Deal!' I said and held out my hand for Alvaro to shake.

We had bought a new car in Spain; on our own!

◆ ◆ ◆

CHAPTER 26: BRITISH BUREAUCRACY

There had been a lot of discussion as to whether our driving licences would be valid in the EU if we left without a Brexit deal, and we took the advice of one of the travel experts on the TV and decided to spend £11 each on an International Driving Licence.

We quickly learned that requirements for these documents were different for Spain than most of Europe, so if we needed to drive through France, we would need two different ones each.
We made the decision just to buy those relevant for use in Spain at this stage. We didn't foresee a situation where we would be driving to Almazara any time soon, and the need for these documents

may turn out to be just a bit more Brexit nonsense that we might never use anyway.

Living as we do in rural Norfolk, we aren't well served with post offices that can issue documents like these, and our efforts to find one that could help us led us to Wroxham, in the heart of the Norfolk Broads. The post office there said they were sure they could help us, although, they admitted, they'd never actually done it before.

As ever we had a trip planned when the news that we should get International Driving Licences hit the headlines, and we had very little time to get them organised. We gathered up all the information we thought we would need to purchase the licences but discovered we needed passport style photographs and found that the nearest one of those booths that take them for you was in a supermarket, ten miles away from the post office.

When we'd got that done and gone to the issuing post office, the process was lengthy and halting as each of the three members of staff consulted each other on each step and tried to remember their training.

The licences themselves were first issued in 1949 and were still printed on that old-fashioned cardboard they used for the original car log books or ration cards. It was obvious from the typeface and the style that they hadn't been revised since the original issue and had been hastily reprinted as part of the Brexit panic.

There was some confusion as to which of the little rubber 'Department for Transport' stamps should be applied and where, to indicate which classes of vehicles we were entitled to drive, but at last it was done and we each had a little grey cardboard International Driving Permit which was valid for just one year, after which we would have to repeat the exercise all over again.

The UK is catching up with the long-winded nature of Spanish bureaucracy, it seems!

We would probably never need to produce these archaic things, and we chuckled as we imagined what the Spanish police would make of them if we ever had to produce them, but at least we were legal; £22 poorer (thank you Brexit), but legal.

CHAPTER 27: NEW TYRES, ANYONE?

We were disappointed at how badly the new car had been prepared for our collection by the garage when we picked it up.
Yes, they had serviced it and given it a wash, but there were used tissues in the door bins and the interior was still quite dusty.
Obviously there had been some sort of a hiatus when we turned up to collect it at the allotted time and found it wasn't ready.

Alvaro, the salesman, wasn't happy.

'The car is unready,' he announced as the meet-and-greet girl showed us to his desk.
'The mechanic, he say need new tyres. I very sad, we lose much money now on this car.'

After something of an explanation was extracted, it emerged that when the car had been put

through the workshop to be prepared for our collection, it was discovered that the tyres were damaged, but that they had no suitable tyres in stock and had to send out for them. This caused the delay.
As Alvaro went off to deal with another customer and the meet-and-greet girl departed without succeeding in pressing refreshments on us once again, I began to think about what had been said.

'Hang on,' I growled to Bee, 'this is a Ford Main Dealership! They must have tyres in stock for a Ford Fiesta, surely! What's all this nonsense about having to order them in?'

Bee rolled her eyes.

'You don't honestly think they're going to give us the sort of expensive tyres new cars come with, do you?' she asked. 'No, they've sent out for some cheapo ones, and that's what's causing the delay.'

It made perfect sense, of course.
'Well I hope they hurry up. We have to fly home in the morning.'

Alvaro at last appeared with the keys and paperwork, but he looked as if he was about to burst into tears.
'Is bad, bad. I make such a bad deal. We make big loss on this car. Choo got bargain, but I got big trouble.' And he shook his head in dismay as he

handed the keys over and I gave him the paperwork and keys for Gwen.

With a final sigh, Alvaro showed us to the car and, although in the UK I would have spent time going over it, it was late, the garage was closing and we were keen to be on our way, so we drove off without further comment.

In the morning, as we drove the car out of our garage ready to load it up with our cases, we got our first proper look at it, but it was too late to complain now, so we cleared out the used tissues and dusted it off where we could and headed off.
To be fair it was actually a nice car which drove very well, and it was a very pleasant change from the noisy, slow, cramped conditions in Gwen. It went up the hills beautifully too.

We'd arranged to store the car in a sort of warehouse near the airport, where the company that ran it would put the battery on a charger (which we had to supply), and arrange to take us to and from the airport in their rattling minibus as many times a year as we needed, in return for an annual fee.
It wasn't bad value either, about the same for a year as nine or ten weeks would have cost to leave a car in a field near Stanstead airport in the UK. They would even wash the car for us each time we collected it for a couple of euros more.

The weather was awful when we landed at Alicante airport when we went to pick the car up some weeks later. It was also the first time Bee was to drive the new car.

I don't know why, but for some reason the driving normally falls to me, but I struggle in the dark and will avoid driving at night if at all possible. So, as our flight arrived at quite a late hour on this occasion, the driving was down to Bee.

It doesn't rain much in Spain, and if your car is kept indoors most of the time, the windscreen wipers are rarely needed. They were needed on this night, however, and how!
It was as though someone had undone a zip in the sky and stood back while all the built-up rain poured out at once. We'd experienced these torrential downpours a couple of times before in Spain but luckily hadn't had to drive in one until now, but after hasty stowing of the luggage, we were ready to be on our way.

'Any idea how you turn the wipers on?' Bee had mastered the lights and adjusted the seat and mirrors already.
When she found the control, the wipers moved up from their dusty hiding place and emerged into the elements. The one on the passenger side split, leaving a trailing piece of rubber flapping with each sweep. 'Good job it's only that one,' I said as

we turned onto the motorway and the satnav told us to proceed on this road for 85 kilometres. That seemed to be the signal the other one was waiting for, and as the rain seemed to come down even harder as our speed increased, it also split and started flapping about.

What Bee said next is best not recorded, but suffice it to say that it wasn't the most relaxing journey to mark the start of our next stay in sunny Spain.

CHAPTER 28: UP THE HILLS WE GO!

Now that we have a reliable car that can cope with the hills, (and with new windscreen wipers too) we occasionally set off for a bit of an explore.

We'd found some truly stunning viewpoints high up on the cliffs, overlooking the sea, which, just as in the travel brochures, really is that colour.
One such discovery we made was Cabo San Antonio, on the end of the Montgo mountain range, which is a national park, from which you can see for miles around.

This little promontory is 160 metres above sea level and features a lighthouse set high up on the tops of the cliffs with views to Jávea one way and Denia the other. I'm told you can see Ibiza and even Mallorca on a clear day from this spot, and it makes a delightful day out with various walks and nature trails to explore.

There are campsites off the approach road to this spot where backpackers can set up tents under the trees and commune with nature. Mind you, I wouldn't fancy it in a wind.

This National Park area, I'm told, is blessed with some wonderful flora and fauna including, according to the blurb, "kermes oak, red lavender, maritime fennel, rockrose, the Valencia rock violet, the rock scabious, the black sabine and the palmetto".

In terms of fauna you might see "the yellow legged seagull or Audouin gull, several types of crow, ravens and birds of prey such as the partridge eagle, royal owls, kestrels and the pilgrim falcon." I'm not sure 'partridge eagle' isn't a typo in the Spanish literature, but if not it might explain the rapid decline of the species, and the 'pilgrim falcon' may also have questions to answer!

There are also foxes, rabbits and genet wild cats (although for all I know these might be feral domesticated moggies), along with various types of reptiles, amphibians, and more peaceable birds like the funny hoopoe, bee-eaters, and swallows. I'm no bird watcher, but Bee finds plenty of interest here.

I was also told that there are wild boar living nearby, but have never seen them or their enchanting 'humbug' striped young.

The local authorities try very hard to protect this wild heritage and won't permit trips of more than ten persons at a time without prior notification, although how they police that in such a large wild area I can't imagine.

There are rare orchids and some plants which are so threatened they grow only here, which I could tell you more about if my Spanish was better, but all but one of the guidebooks, maps, and pamphlets we've found to date on this area are in Spanish without an English translation.

Still, I guess that underlines that this is where the Spanish go on holiday; but I hope they'll forgive me for recommending a trip out to this spot which you can enjoy with or without the literature.
Just don't forget the sensible shoes and plenty of water as this is wild country with no water fountains or other tourist aids.

On another of our little excursions, we came across a place where all the sand on the beach had washed away, exposing the bedrock.

Apparently this was the result of a man-made accident, for which read politically motivated cock-

up, caused by an attempt to alter the course of a river some way further inland. The result of this ill-conceived idea left this little holiday town, popular it seems with German
expats, without a beach and with a distinctively unattractive seaside area.

The beach apparently washed away over a couple of weeks when the sluices made to control the new waterways were opened, and it will now take years and many millions to restore the status quo, if they ever do succeed in doing it.

It's slightly surreal to drive into what is obviously a seaside town with holiday flats, beach cafés, and bars as well as shops selling buckets and spades, to find that its principle attraction to holiday-makers has literally washed away.

There are notice boards explaining what happened and the vast project they propose to undertake to put it right at the end of the road to where the beach was, but they're faded and decaying, and I can't help but wonder whether the authorities will ever be able to raise the money or the political motivation to put this right.

At the other end of the scale, a few kilometres away lies Jávea, very much a thriving beach destination, popular with Brits and other Europeans. It features a picturesque but mostly extremely crowded sandy beach known as the Arenal. This little gem is flanked by up-market bars, restaurants, and beach shops in profusion on a wide tiled promenade that stretches the length of the beach. Delightful though that may be, it's certainly not all there is to Jávea.

The town is divided into three sections; the Arenal beach area, the port, and the more inland old town. Each has its own charms including, we discovered, a splendid restaurant set over the first and second floors of a building with uninterrupted views in the port area, a vibrant market in the old town, and some really good eateries in the Arenal, including a British run vegan restaurant, and to entice the expats further, Indian and burger bar options.

In some parts of the town, including the beach area, you can even park for free, which makes it very popular, as you might imagine. Pretty it may be, but in season it's a magnet for holidaymakers, so peaceful it is not.

◆ ◆ ◆

CHAPTER 29: MOORS AND CHRISTIANS

All the Spanish seem to go on holiday in August, and quite a few of them appear to like to descend on our stretch of coastline. The influx of people makes the population of the towns and villages swell for a few weeks, and there are fiestas and festivals aplenty to keep them entertained.

One such is the annual Moors & Christians event which takes place at other times of the year in other areas, but is one of the highlights of August here. The background to this historic event is well documented elsewhere so I shan't bore you with a history lesson, suffice to say, according to Wikipedia, that the festival commemorates the battles, combats and fights between the Moors (i.e. Muslims) and Christians during the period known as the Reconquista (from the 8th through to the 15th century). We went along, of course, although not for the full week of celebrations, mock battles, and revelry, and we were completely amazed by what we saw.

The spectacle, the sumptuousness and intricacies of the costumes, the fascinating floats, complete with fire-breathing dragons, the dancers, the marching bands, the horse-riding display, and the delightful tableaux put on by children telling ancient tales were marvellous. And the procession went on and on and on.
Considering the size of the town, albeit that it draws participants from surrounding villages which swell the numbers, and the fact that this is something they've been doing for centuries, not as some polished tourist thing, makes this huge event absolutely magnificent.

It's enjoyed by visitors to the town, of course, but it's not put on *for* visitors to the town; although if you ask me, with so many participants in the main event, most of the population must be taking part in it rather than watching.

We learned that participating was a great honour, and that the multitudes of marching bands (containing young and old alike) practice all year, while children perfect dances which are set sequences of the history being portrayed.

The vast floats with all kinds of mechanical wonders attached must have taken months and lots of money to create.
The dancing horses were followed by a camel, and each of them was followed by a street cleaner with a trolley and a shovel, just in case. No doubt the sandal-wearing partici pants in their regimented arms-linked lines were pleased to see him!

Like most of the big events, it went on in various forms for days, was extremely noisy, and involved copious amounts of eating and drinking, all topped off with fireworks and no doubt quite a few sore heads.

If you get a chance to go to a Moors & Christians event, don't miss it. But take some water and be prepared to be pelted by boiled sweets, flung principally for the children from each of the floats as the cigar smoking much be-weaponed 'soldiers' shuffle by.

CHAPTER 30: FIESTA!

One of the disadvantages of being on a mountain when you walk with a stick is that you tire quickly. However, there's something about Spain that improves things. Perhaps it's the dry air. The drizzle, mizzle, and general sogginess of the climate in the UK gets into the bones, and for me at least, means gradual seizing up in the winter months.

I have a persistent but generally well controlled back condition, which will flare up occasionally but for a good proportion of the time, is manageable. It will never get better, but it's certainly easier when we are in Spain in the warm.

In the UK, when I was in my teens and early twenties, I ran hospital radio and mobile discos, and danced the night away regularly without a second thought.

The student nurses at the local hospital...well, let's draw a veil over that. Those days are in the dead past and probably better left there!

Suffice it to say that nowadays, when it comes to dancing, I leave it to Bee.
That was, until the night of the Almazara Fiesta!

The Spanish love a party, and the louder and later the better. Our little urbanisation even puts on its own fiesta each year.

We'd been in Spain soaking up the warmth for a couple of weeks before this event and, although I want to make it clear that we're not the sort that sunbathe for hours (something I regard as the most boring and wasteful thing you can do with a sunny day), the sun had soaked into my old bones, and I was feeling terrific.

We'd been invited to take folding chairs (we'd discovered there were two of those uncomfortable things with the low seats in the store, under the piles of rubbish) with wine and picnic stuff to meet a group of people in a spot they reserve every year under the trees, on a raised area of grass in the best position to enjoy the music at the fiesta.

We felt rather honoured to be invited to join this group, which was attended by Peter and Holly of course, a couple of other British couples, two German couples, and a French family as well a variety of local householders from all over the world who seemed to visit the seated group to pay their respects in a rolling procession. Those present in our little group included the event organisers.

The idea was to arrive early to claim our spot before the fiesta got underway, and arrange picnic rugs and folding chairs by about 7:30 p.m., while the stage, made out of the trailers of two elderly lorries, was constructed and the sound system was being set up.

The stage was set up across the road and blocked it off completely, which created a dancing area on the road in front of it.
This sort of behaviour is quite normal in Spain apparently and goes on all the time when they fancy a party.
This little road might not be the M25, but it would mean quite a detour for any unsuspecting drivers who were not aware of the event.

In Spain, all events, even children's parties, start much later than you might expect so that the heat has time to go out of the sun, and as the sunset gives way to darkness, everyone is much cooler and ready for some energetic revelling.
As the bar was being set up under the pine trees, we were already tucking into round one of our pic-

nics and on the second glass of Cava from the cool-box.

This was desperately early to be eating in Spain, and we had a long night ahead of us, so the general consensus at this stage was to just have nibbles and chatter as we got to know each other before the music got too loud.
It was great to swap stories about how we'd each come to be in Almazara, but the common thread was that we all loved it and enjoyed life there enormously. Some of the group were full-time residents, some were regular holiday makers, and some, like us, were nomads, spending whatever time we could here and treasuring every moment.

Everyone sat or stood wherever they liked as we talked, with no territorial guarding of 'our' chairs as everything was shared. The low folding chairs we'd brought along were incredibly difficult to get out of on the uneven ground, and much amusement was had when I discovered that the only way I could escape to stand up was to roll sideways out of them onto the grass. The first time, I nearly knocked a wine bottle flying but caught it before any damage, or more importantly, spillage occurred, and from then on, anyone who sat on these contraptions suffered pretty much the same fate.

'They're going in the bin when this is over,' I muttered to Bee as another of the group rolled out of one of them, legs akimbo, and we weren't even drunk yet!

First up on the makeshift stage was a traditional flamenco guitarist who started slowly and sent out gentle wave like sounds to set the tone for this part of the evening. He was soon joined by his son, who had one of those clever electric drum boxes that you sit on like a stool and tap out a beat. He produced a more modern vibe for his father to play to, and then mum and sister joined the throng in full flamenco dresses and things started to hot up as they gave it their best.

They weren't bad at all, although dad was definitely the star turn, and his energy was something to see.

When they took a break, it was getting dark, and we moved on to pizza slices and more Cava from the coolbox as the band started to test their light show and the sound system; and promptly blew out all the power.
It was soon fixed, however, and we started to feel the vibrations as they belted out their first couple

of numbers.

As the remains of the cheese was unceremoniously dumped back in the coolbox with all the wrappings, and as the last bottle was opened, some of the children were dancing and a handful of the adults started to join them.
The Brits did the 'self-conscious shuffle' while a Spanish couple threw themselves into an energetic Lindy-hop routine, which looked very professional.

The band were good, and as the midnight hour approached, the dance floor/road was full of dancers. But now the Cava was gone, and even the emergency bottle of plonk we'd brought along just in case, was history and the contents of the coolbox were long forgotten.

Deep down I began to remember the joy of making a fool of myself on the dance floor, and as my foot tapped and the last of the wine went down, I put down my stick and stepped up to join the growing throng.

Bee, probably thinking I might fall over, followed me down the shallow steps onto the road/dance floor, and as the band turned the pace of the music up a bit to 80s disco with a song we knew, we found that we were dancing!

I waggled a mean shoe in my day...no, alright, I just

jiggled about like everyone else did back then, but tonight it all came back. I was one with the beat. I was lost in music. I had lost my heart to a starship trooper, and Mamma Mia, could I ring my bell!
I may not have been the greatest dancer, but I attempted the 'disco dad' with some determination and throughly enjoyed myself.

Unsurprisingly the next day it took two attempts to get out of bed and three cups of coffee before the brain cleared. The night before, Bee had tut-tutted and expounded at length about how I would regret it and be curled up in a ball for a week afterwards, but I was functioning pretty well.

It had to be the Spain effect, although next time we saw Peter, he did rather tease!

CHAPTER 31: IT'LL WASH OUT

Bee and I love trying different places to eat and the *Ruta de Tapas* could have been made for us.

This annual event encourages people to visit bars and restaurants all over the nearby town to try tapas with a beer, a wine, or a glass of vermouth, for just €3.00 a go.

We discovered some great places during this event and felt much more connected with the town as a result. The idea is that, with a little booklet as your guide, you try to visit new places and get a taste of what they have to offer. It's a great advertisement for the restaurants and a great adventure for the participants.

In each place we visited, an often really elegant and delicious tapa was served with a drink, and the establishment stamped our little book.

There was an additional incentive to get round all the places taking part in the form of a competition with a prize but, as there were about 40 restaurants and bars taking part over a wide area, we knew we were never going to get round them all in the time available to us, try as we might.

We did notice that there was a great spirit of competition between the bars and restaurants themselves, trying to out-do each other to win their own prize as much as to show off their capabilities to customers old and new.

The quality of what was on offer was unbelievable. Real thought had gone into each dish, and the cooks had gone to great lengths to design tapa which were as pleasing to the eye as they were to the palette. Of course from their point of view this was the best advertisement they could get, and if we liked what we saw, we were much more likely to return for a full meal.

They clearly made little or no money on what they served on this occasion, but the profile raising opportunity was not to be missed. It worked too. Several of the places we discovered on the *Ruta de Tapas* have become firm favourites for us, and we return to them regularly.

Of course everyone's taste is different, and there were a couple of places we decided were not for us and we haven't been back; but at least we went and tried them out, which was the whole point after all.

I did have a rather unfortunate incident at one place which, as it happened, we really rather liked, when visiting again.
On this occasion I was dining alone as Bee had returned to the UK to work, and I sat outside at a shady table with a view between the pine trees to the Mediterranean. I ordered spaghetti bolognese and sat back with a large glass of cold beer ready to enjoy my lunch in the almost empty restaurant.

A dish of olives arrived along with some fresh bread and a pot of garlic mayonnaise (*pan y alioli*), but the wait for the main course wasn't long. A vast bowl arrived with a smaller one containing grated hard cheese, and I licked my lips. The spaghetti was steaming, but unfortunately the bolognese in the middle was cold.

I called over the waitress and explained the situation in my halting Spanish.
'Er, *pardone, camerera.* Um, it's *frío,*' I tried.

'Ees cold? Oh, I so sorry, I change for fresh!' and off she went.

The dish was obviously being prepared anew and not just bunged in the microwave, as it took some time to come back. I ordered another big beer and was informed once again that they were very sorry, offered me more bread, and assured me my meal would not be long.

Eventually the waitress emerged with an even larger bowl held aloft which, tripping as she approached my table, she upended and spilled all over me, the table, and the terrace!

Amid the gasps, repeated apologies, and furious mopping, a small dog at the next table couldn't believe his luck, and eventually had to be picked up to restrain him from licking the terrace clean of all traces of the ruins.

The waitress would accept no payment for the third bowl, or the by now three large beers and side dishes I'd enjoyed, and to the sound of further apologies, I teetered home, happy and replete, with a mission to find and understand the washing machine instructions.

CHAPTER 32: DECISIONS? MAÑANA!

In the background, both before and after we bought our apartment, Bee and I had always been wrestling with the issue of how we intended to use it.
We decided early on that we weren't going to rent it out on the holiday market. The rules on letting had tightened up and the setup costs as well as the commission payments were prohibitive. The apartment was just too special to us. We didn't want to share it with anyone.

Holiday lets might have been the practical and prudent route to follow, and having rented an apartment for a fortnight not far away, we were well aware of the sort of income we were turning our backs on. However, that decision was made,

and the main issue for us related to when Bee finally retired.
Would we spend a few weeks, a few months, or even most of the year in Spain?

Bee wasn't convinced that she wanted to move to Spain full time, and I favoured the idea of six months spent in each country, probably in two or three month long sections. But nothing was decided.

We now knew what was involved in driving over as well as how easy or difficult it was to fly, and we understood the costs involved and the issues relating to the dog.
These decisions would have been simpler if the dog was calmer and easier to live with, but he was with us for his lifetime, and there were no easy fixes in terms of how to include him in our plans.

We'd looked into ferries, but our attempts to book a trip from the UK to Santander or Bilbao left us confused, and in the end we gave up on that idea, at least as far as booking a sailing to take the dog with us. It seemed however far in advance we tried to book, all the dog-friendly cabins or kennels were sold out whenever we could go.
Perhaps that would be different once Bee had retired and we could avoid the school holidays, but we would have to wait and see.

Obviously we couldn't take Barkley with us on

aeroplanes, and we were starting to feel guilty about leaving him behind. The cost of kennels, when we had to use them, cancelled out the effect of cheap air fares, and no doubt made the cost of getting to Almazara equivalent to driving or going on a ferry.
We even looked into buying a camper van to reduce the stress of travelling or staying in hotels with the dog, but we couldn't really justify the cost.

Meanwhile it was cattle class on the jet planes for us, and we endured all the usual privations to use them.

As Bee's retirement date approached and we knew that, at last, we could unshackle our travel arrangements from the dreaded school holidays, we looked forward to a much greater freedom to decide how we spent our time. But we hadn't made any firm decisions, and if we were honest with ourselves, we were putting it off.

That's not to say we weren't enjoying ourselves in the meantime. We visited castles and monuments, attended festivals and fiestas, planned a trip to Granada to see the Alhambra, and discussed how we could use the apartment as a base to explore more of Europe.

But Brexit was rumbling on.
There were uncertainties about air travel and pet

passports, and even talk of visas. The deadline for our departure from the EU came and went with nothing at all resolved; and all that was really negotiated was an extension of time. The corrosive effect on the Pound, British industry, and the wider economy was beginning to become clearer, and, as the pundits counted up the billions spent or lost so far, without even having left yet, a mood of depression settled on the UK.

With our international aspirations and now responsibilities, we were not immune from all this worry, and I nervously watched the news and political programmes for clues as to what on earth all this was going to mean for us.

'Staycations' became a thing. The holidaying British didn't want to invest much and elected not to spend on holidays abroad (daft, as even with the kids, we'd always found it was much more expensive to stay in the UK than take a trip abroad), and confidence seeped away as Brexit dragged on and on.

Despite having a bolthole in Spain, we weren't immune from the general downturn the UK had brought upon itself, and we worried whether the dreadfully low interest rates would ever rise, so that we could stop eating our savings. All these factors stopped us making decisions about how much time we would be spending in Spain.

But hey, travelling is supposed to be fun, isn't it? So we didn't let all that baggage, if you will excuse the pun, hold us back, and we were soon planning our next trip.

CHAPTER 33: A VILLA TOO FAR?

As you might expect, were concerned that all this flying backwards and forwards wasn't doing anything positive for our green footprint.

Teasingly Bee justified our air flights by saying each plane contained a lot of people who might otherwise be driving a whole lot of polluting cars to do the same journey; and that may, or may not, be a reasonable approach, but having never set foot on an aeroplane until my late twenties, I thought I had some catching up to do with some of the frequent flyers we met who seemed to fly every other weekend.

There was no doubt, however, that staying put for longer in one place was desirable, and once Bee retired and our time was our own, we knew that we could, and perhaps should, change our arrangements. We discussed it constantly.

Our conversations were fuelled on occasions by my irresistible attraction to the website Kyero, which much like the British Rightmove, constantly updates with property coming onto the market and, it has to be said, less frequently, being sold.

We had met a charming British estate agent called Angela and been impressed with the number of times her company seemed to be involved in selling property on our urbanisation, on the mountain, and nearby.

She was relaxed but also industrious and competent, and as she drove the same make and model of sports car I had in the UK, we had found conversation, with a shared interest, easy.

One warm afternoon as we sat on the terrace of the local bar, overlooking the tennis club, she arrived and, dropping her tennis racket on the ground, slumped down into a chair at an adjacent table.
She smiled a greeting, exclaimed that she was getting too old for tennis lessons, and asked how we were settling in.

The conversation flowed lightly back and forth as the restorative cold drinks had the desired effect, and we mentioned our dilemma about spending more time in Almazara once Bee retired.

Now Angela is charming and not at all pushy, but she does have a job to do, and she could never be accused of not spotting an opportunity when it presented itself.
Perhaps unwisely I mentioned my obsession with Kyero searches, and she laughed and said it was a very common disease. But what was the harm?

'Did you see that really nice little villa I put on there the day before yesterday, just over the road from here?' she asked. 'You can almost see it from here, and it's got a rooftop terrace with pretty much the same view as from your place.'
'Was that the one with the plunge pool?' I asked. 'Whatever *is* a plunge pool?'
'I'll show you,' she smiled, and before we knew it, we'd arranged to meet her outside the villa the very next day.

The description of this particular little villa on the website had rather caught my eye. Apart from the mysterious plunge pool, it had a garden on three sides, off-road parking behind a gate, under a cover of sorts, a couple of bedrooms, and a good-sized lounge with a reasonable view towards the sea.
The icing on the cake, in the form of a roof terrace, was further enhanced by an outdoor kitchen for

those balmy evening cookouts...I was beginning to sound like an estate agent myself...but the price seemed reasonable too.

Obviously Angela was under no illusions that we were in any position to buy at present and realised we would have to sell at least one property to buy another, but she explained that she had to take some better photographs of the property anyway, so why not join her for a nosy round.

All the roads on the mountain are pleasantly hedged with oleander, hibiscus, and bougainvillaea, and the little road to this villa was no exception. The neatly kept gardens and driveways told of well maintained property within, and whilst this short road contained much smaller houses than the more prolific 'millionaires villas', it was all very pleasant.

Angela, camera in hand, was leaning on her sports car when we arrived.
She'd already unlocked and opened the gate which led to the driveway, with a little outhouse on the right and the villa on the left.
'What's in there?' I asked, pointing at the outhouse.
'Oh, that's a workshop. The old gentleman who lived here made things, it seems,' and she unlocked the door and pushed it open.
The building was about two thirds the size of a

single garage with a high ceiling and walls covered in racks of woodworking tools. There was a substantial bench, a wood lathe, some cupboards, and the floor was strewn with wood shavings.
'Looks like he's been pretty busy,' I said. 'Does he still live here?'
'No, he's had to go and live with relatives as he was getting a bit elderly to live on his own.' Angela smiled, 'Come and look at the villa.'

A wide bougainvillaea covered porch, which was crying out for a couple of rocking chairs, led to the front door, which opened straight into the lounge.

There was an open fireplace with a substantial chimney breast along one wall and windows on two sides which, when Angela opened the shutters, revealed a pleasant outlook over a compact but shady garden. The kitchen was disappointingly small and in need of a re-fit, and the bedrooms, opening straight off the lounge, were also quite cramped. Still, over all it was quite attractive, if in need of some TLC, and it would make an ideal holiday home for someone.

Outside there were various covered areas with plastic roofing used in abundance. Unfortunately the sun had done a lot of damage to these areas, and the plastic was brittle and broken in places.

The roof terrace, however, was lovely, and although lower down the mountain so not blessed with quite such a broad a view as from our own place, it still had a good outlook towards the Mediterranean.

'Very nice,' I said, 'but where is this plunge pool?'

Angela, who'd been clicking away with her camera, stopped what she was doing.

'Oh, I'd almost forgotten that. Follow me!'

Up a few steps to a raised area of garden behind the workshop, there was a rockery and a glass fibre cover over an area about the size of three domestic bath tubs.

'Can you give me a hand with this?' Angela asked as she grasped one of the handles mounted on the cover.

As we lifted it, a cloud of flies burst out, and what was revealed was a rather grubby jacuzzi, set into the ground, and obviously unused for quite some time.

'Yuck!' Bee grimaced as the cover was hastily replaced.

'Hmm,' said Angela. 'My colleague did the details on this one. I think I'll have to amend the plunge pool words!'

We thanked Angela for letting us have a look round and left her taking pictures of the view.

'At least you now have an idea of what you could buy if you did decide to spend more time over here,' she said. 'See you soon.'
A seed had definitely been sown.

CHAPTER 34: THE BEST LAID PLANS...

As the day for Bee's retirement drew closer, we made all sorts of plans. Then finally the great day was here.

As a retirement present, the management and the lovely staff of the nursery school clubbed together and paid for both of us to go to see a show in London - *The Lion King* stage show - which was high on Bee's bucket list, and we started to look forward to our trips abroad.
We also got busy booking flights and planning for the number one thing on Bee's bucket list - a safari in Africa.

Then, as with all the best laid plans, the brakes were slammed on when I became ill.

During our trip to London to see the show, I began

to feel quite unwell, and while I said nothing at the time so as not to spoil the event, the next day I was on the phone to the doctor as I felt really poorly.

Sod's law being what it is, by the time I'd convinced the doctor's receptionist that I actually did need to see a doctor and she'd generously allowed me to make a ten minute appointment for a couple of weeks' time, the symptoms had cleared up a bit, but I was still quite unwell.

It seemed prudent, given the sort of tests I was subsequently being sent for, to plan our safari trip for the following year, and I bought the travel agent's no doubt hideously overpriced insurance to cover the cost, just in case.

However the hospital consultant pronounced me, if not fit, at least well enough to travel to Spain, so off we went as planned.

It seemed our return was not a moment too soon.

There was water on the floor in the utility room and the plug-in-timer for the water heater, which we always unplugged when away, was swimming in a puddle on top of the washing machine.

The culprit, we quickly discovered, was the wall mounted electric water heater, which had sprung what appeared to be a slow leak, dripping onto the washing machine beneath it. This temperamental device had, until now, heated water when it felt like it and not when it didn't.

It was clearly on its last legs anyway, but as with many of these things, *mañana* had got us, and we'd ignored it a bit too long.

We mopped up and decided to waste no more time in visiting the *electrodomésticos* in the nearby town that had served us so well when we needed a new washing machine.

These water heaters consist of a large white painted cylinder which hangs on the wall and gurgles away to itself with a built-in immersion heater and thermostat. On ours there was a handy dial that was intended to indicate the approximate water temperature.
It had always steadfastly refused to move from the halfway point, and as a result, until we bought the plug-in-timer to control it, there was never enough hot water when we needed it, or there was a full tank if we were going out for the day.

It had obviously seen better days.

'So,' I asked, as the nice English speaking lady concluded her demonstrations of the two or three models available, 'can you fit it for us?'

'No, I sorry, you must get a plumber.'
'That´s awkward,' Bee said. 'Still we could call

Denilo when we got home. He'll know what to do.'

We decided to visit the almost adjacent builder's merchants while we were there. Our holiday money was going to be severely dented by this little exercise, so we may as well see if this place had cheaper ones, we reasoned.

It did, and half an hour later we were queuing at the checkout with a huge box on a trolley containing what promised to be a 'Digital Smart Water Heater', which, it seemed, was a direct replacement for our old one but featured 'Smart Technology' to make it more economical to run, and a little digital display in a window showing the temperature and (I thought) a timer.

I've never learned to 'keep it simple, stupid' and I wasn't going to start now!

We called Denilo and, sure enough, within a couple of hours there he was.

The view from our apartment really is lovely. Straight ahead we have the wide sweep of the Mediterranean, where, looking over the rooftops of the nearby town, we can pick out sailing and fishing boats close in to shore and massive ships on the horizon, as well as Ibiza and on a clear day even the outline of Mallorca.

Slightly to the right, we look down the fairways of the beautifully kept golf course and are protected from the weather by the dominant presence of The Montgo mountain and nature reserve which changes colour from steely grey to the brightest orange continually as the sun tracks across the sky.

To the left, a little further away, another mountain provides a spectacular backdrop to the sunset and, with our own mountain in the middle, completes three sides of a wide bay open to the sea on the fourth side. We look across hectares of orange groves, which have a lovely scent, vines, almond and avocado groves, all dotted with stands of olive trees.

We rarely see any aircraft in the usually clear blue sky, except the little fire spotters and water-carrying helicopters if there is a fire, and any jets we do see are very high up so we can't hear them and are only aware of them if we see a vapour trail. We do also occasionally see private helicopters delivering the well-heeled for a round of golf coming in to land below us, and very occasionally one of our neighbours flies his helicopter to his house higher up the mountain, but other than that all is calm and quiet.

It really is remarkably peaceful here. The mountains must deflect the sounds as, on the other side of 'our' mountain, the motorway is only a couple of miles away, but we've never heard it or any traffic apart from our neighbours' cars coming and going, and if the wind is in the right direction, we might dimly hear the occasional shout of 'Four!' from the golf course below when a ball is miss-hit.

I can't claim that our view to the Med is completely unobstructed because a little lower down the mountain there is a row of houses with roof terraces which sit just below our balcony level, but because the mountain is very steep at this point and the architect has cleverly used the fall to set the properties below each other, these houses don't hamper our outlook too badly.

I particularly like to look at the ever-changing colours in the mountains above the verdant woods where the trees thin out towards the peak. The scene is never the same twice, and the bird life up there is enchanting.

But we can't sit about admiring the view all day. Here's Denilo with his assessment of what is to be done about the water heater.

'Eees not a big job, but we need drain the water,' he

announced. 'Have choo buckets?'

We had two, and Denilo organised us into a sort of a chain gang to empty the thing.
Bee was on the sink end, pouring away the water. I was in the middle, and Denilo swapped the rapidly filling buckets as the old tank disgorged it contents.

The weather over the last couple of days had improved considerably and this, even with all the windows open, proved hot work. Denilo positively dripped but refused all refreshment.
'Can't stop it now! It not take long.'

It was surprising how long it did take and how much water the thing seemed to hold, but eventually it slowed to a trickle, and preparations were made to install the new one. After a trip to the store to buy longer flexible pipes to connect it, it was done, and Denilo pronounced that it was time to switch it on and try it out.

I'd been reading the instructions while Denilo worked and established that the little display window only showed the temperature of the water and which of the three programmes the unit was set to. There was no timer, or any external connections, so how this thing claimed to be 'smart' was a little unclear.

The taps spluttered and coughed, and the little

display lit up and informed us it was in 'smart mode' and that the temperature was currently 22 degrees.

The instructions said that, '*After a period of learning*', the unit would '*adjust itself the hot water temperature adapted to the user consumption.*'
The instructions may not have had entirely the best translation into English, but I think the meaning was clear when it said, '*This allows an optimisation of the electrical consumption.*'

That evening we left it in 'smart mode' as per the instructions and went to bed.

In the morning the little screen had misted over, and as far as I could make out, read '*00*'.
The water was absolutely scalding hot, and we discovered it leaked!

'This is no good,' said Bee crossly as I called Denilo. 'And how on earth do you turn the wretched thing down?'

But you couldn't turn it down. The screen stubbornly refused to respond to repeated button pressing, and it simply boiled and leaked, no matter what we did.
Denilo called three times to try to stop it leaking. Fortunately it wasn't leaking much, but eventually we had to concede that it was not the connections he made that were at fault but the unit itself

which seemed to weep where the cold water went in.

We would have to take it back.

We turned it off to let it cool down and repeated the draining operation as before.

'We're going to have a hell of a big water bill,' I said gloomily as another bucket of still-hot water went down the sink, 'and if it's been boiling all night, I hate to wonder what the electricity bill is going to be.'

Denilo and I put the tank in his car and took it back to the store. We hoped they would exchange it, as obviously we still needed a means of heating the water; or at least give us our money back.

Denilo acted as translator and explained the situation at the customer care desk. He asked first if we could have a replacement.

'No.'

'Why not?' I asked, and Denilo, after a sharp intake of breath as he listened to the answer, translated.

'She say we cannot exchange because the unit has been installed.'

'Hang on,' I said, 'how on earth are you supposed to find out if it's faulty if you don't install it?'

The customer care assistant shrugged.

‘Well, can we have our money back then?’

‘No.’
‘Why not?’
Denilo translated again. ‘She say we not get refund because we have installed the unit.’

Further probing by Denilo revealed that the only course of action open to us was to call the manufacturer who would send someone out to look at it in an undisclosed timescale, and if he was satisfied that the unit had a fault that wasn’t caused by us, he would arrange for us to return it to the store and collect another one.

There were, of course, two major problems with this. The first was that we needed hot water today, not in some unspecified timescale when an inspector had called. The second problem was that we were due to fly home in a few days and wouldn’t be around for about six weeks after that to receive an inspector at our apartment.

‘How long does it take an inspector to come?’ Denilo asked.
The customer care assistant shrugged, said she had no idea, and turned to deal with another customer.
‘There is nothing for it, Denilo,’ I said, ‘we will

have to buy another one and fight it out with the manufacturer to get a refund later.'

'*Sí*,' nodded Denilo 'Maybe we buy one a bit more simple this time?'
So we bought a basic one and, having extracted yet more euros from us, the customer care individual offered us one last parting shot.
'The inspector,' she said, 'will want to see the receipt and the original box.'

The receipt I had, but the enormous box was much too big for us to store, so it went to the dump along with the original old water heater.

Ho hum.

At the point of writing, I'm still fighting this particular battle, with the maker saying we must deal with the store and the store saying we must deal with the maker.

Needless to say I haven't got my money back yet!

CHAPTER 35: ITS NOT ALL SUN AND SANGRIA

When we bumped into other Brits in or around the nearby town, if they recognised our language and engaged us in conversation, their first question was usually to ask where in the UK we are from.

Anthony and Victoria asked this question as we sat outside a little bar one hot afternoon. When they established Bee had family connections in Surrey they delighted in telling us they came from Esher, well, Hersham which is next door, and how much they were looking forward to moving back there.
'The way we see it, old chap,' expanded Anthony, leaning back in his chair, 'all these foreigners don't much like us Brits, and when we finally leave the

damn EU, they might turn against us.'
'Yes,' chipped in Victoria, 'they haven't made us very welcome, and these Spaniards are so rude. Hardly any of them can be bothered to learn to speak English properly, although they all get taught it at school, so I for one will be jolly glad to see the back of them!'

I resisted the temptation to ask if they had bothered to learn to speak Spanish whilst living in their country, but I suspected I could guess the answer.

'So we are selling up and going home.' Anthony picked up the thread.
'Of course the Spanish have made such a mess of their economy that we've lost a lot of money on our house here, and so far the only people we've had round are bloody Spaniards, and they don't have the cash.'

'No,' added Victoria, 'so we'll only be able to afford a small place, maybe a maisonette, in Hersham. But it's such a pretty village, and I don't want to live anywhere else.'

Hersham, for those who don't know, might have been a pretty village in the 1950s and was probably quite pleasant even into the 1980s, but now it's part of the urban sprawl around London and occupied by commuters wanting a thirty-minute train journey to work, and there was no obvious separation from the surrounding suburbs. Every available space had been sold off to developers and filled with yet more identikit homes.

'How long have you lived here?' I asked.

'Oh, let's see. Well, we were out in Kuala Lumpur with the company for fifteen years, and we moved here when we retired. When would that have been, Anthony, dear?'

'It was 2001 if you remember, old girl. It took that thieving Spanish builder two bloody years to finish the house, so we didn't move in properly until 2003.'

'Have you been back to Hersham since?' I asked.

'What? Oh no. Our daughter lives in Manchester, so we go there when we go home. We're so looking forward to going back there though, and we're going over next month to start doing some house hunting.' Victoria bubbled. 'I can't wait to see the old place again!'

'And the bloody agents can't be worse than these charlies here,' rejoined Anthony. 'The ones we had round were blithering idiots, if you ask me. Spoke hardly a word of English and wanted us to sell the place for peanuts, probably to their bloody family members. Thieves the lot of them,' he added. 'God, it's hot today, and this tea is foul. Can't wait to have a proper British cuppa, and some bloody rain would be nice too!'

We left Anthony and Victoria outside the bar and wished them luck with their house hunting.

Perhaps Spain would be a little more Spanish in the future.

CHAPTER 36: WATER AND MANNERS

When we look out across the orange groves and vineyards climbing the base of the mountain in what looks like a giant's staircase, the greenness of the scenery always impresses us.

We know that water and its management are the key to the success of these crops and marvel at the irrigation system, invented by the Moors centuries ago and mostly still in use, which made it all possible.
When you consider that the Moors' conquest of Spain took place in 711 A.D. and, depending on which history books you read, that they hung about for around 800 years, their achievements are still plain to see.

The irrigation channels, or *'acequias'* they built are still visible and working, and the Moors' experience in the deserts of North Africa enabled them to create a system to grow crops which couldn't normally thrive in this climate.
Spain is one of the largest producers of citrus fruits in the world, and València is one of the most important rice-producing centres in Europe because the Moors' ingenuity enabled these things to be grown, and for the land to be farmed reliably.

The Moors created a prosperous civilisation which became successful as a result of their farming methods and engineering skills, and they built things to last. The channels we can see all around us still work well today, and the system for sharing out the water is based on their ideas.

These irrigation channels sit bone dry and dusty most of the time until, maybe once a fortnight, when it's the individual farmer's turn, the water is diverted further upstream by an official, and it flows, for say two hours, to his little farmstead.
This is a big occasion, and no matter what time of the day the water is due, the farmer will be working hard to make the most of it.

Not a drop is wasted, and it's captured in all sorts of tanks and diverted to create small temporary ponds and muddy fields until it soaks away into the grateful soil.

The system obviously works well on the edges of our mountain, and the citrus and olive groves are thriving, whilst right next to our property, the avocados are healthy and prolific.

We have been told that ‘our’ mountain sits on a huge '*deposito*', a cave full of water deep underground created by the retreating glaciers and replenished by rainwater percolating through the rock. The water is, they say, of excellent quality and quite safe to drink.

Whether the discovery or existence of this water was the reason they chose to build on this particular mountain, I cannot say. But it was developed at a time of great optimism and prosperity, and it certainly wasn’t chosen for its ease of construction, as each road had to be blasted out of the solid rock to create a flat area, and each building plot was steep so that the lowest floor had to be built into the hillside. Our own property is two storeys at the front and three at the back, with the lowest level being the garage and store.

To get water to the properties, pipes were drilled down, and a pumping station was built near the top of the mountain to pump it up from the cave and then distribute it down the slopes to the houses. As a result we have excellent water pressure and haven’t experienced a single day without

water (touch wood).
The urbanisation has its own private water company to administer distribution and maintain the infrastructure, which keeps costs reasonable compared to our less fortunate neighbours in many towns.

Of course the agricultural water is also provided for the vineyards, and they in turn produce wine that we make a point of checking out frequently. There are several *bodegas* (wineries) nearby, some of which offer tours and tastings. The locals use them like off-licences and are often seen with all sorts of plastic bottles and even jerrycans to carry home the weekly wine supplies.

Most of the local wine is absolutely *not* plonk, and Spanish wine now stands up against wine from all over the world in terms of quality. But in Spain at least, it remains deliciously cheap, for which we are very grateful. Naturally there are one or two awful wines, but you get that anywhere, and we do try to give the local offerings a place on our table as much as we can.

The grapes in the immediate vicinity are not grown on a massive commercial scale, but in small patches of ground in between the olives and oranges, and I understand the crop is used either for personal consumption or sent to the big processors, much in the way olives are farmed.

It's quite normal for rural Spanish families to make their own wine, and there are often fierce rivalries between neighbours over who creates the best.

You rarely see a Spaniard drunk, but they do drink far more wine and on more occasions throughout the day than we do. It's quite normal for a Spanish manual worker to start his day with coffee with a splash of brandy in it, and to take small glasses of wine or beer throughout the day. The quantities are small, however, and the British habit of drinking pints or sloshing down a whole lot of beer at a sitting simply isn't their way.

At mealtimes the children are also offered drinks, perhaps of watered down wine, as well. They are also expected to behave themselves at the table and engage with the adults in conversation.

It's a well known fact that the Spanish love children and, when out on the town, once the children are out of the toddler stage, they are treated like grownups. The family dress them up smartly and teach them excellent table manners.

You might see the odd one or two running about between the tables late at night in a restaurant, but that's understandable when you consider they've probably had to sit still for some hours in their parents' and grandparents' company while the meal was taken, and they need to let off some steam.

All this is changing with the advent of mobile phones, of course, which as any parent knows, make excellent child minders, but hopefully the Spanish will continue to produce polite well behaved children with great respect for their elders.

They are going to need to, as with a tradition of providing for the older generation within the family, there's limited state or private provision for the care of older people, and there's no welfare state in quite the terms we understand it to fall back on.

Meanwhile, as long as the cheap wine flows and the sun keeps shining, the Spanish economy does well from tourism, and Bee and I continue to contribute our little bit.

CHAPTER 37: THE VILLAGE THAT WON THE LOTTERY

The Spanish love lotteries and operate a complicated system of ticket kiosks in every town often manned by, and designed to give employment to, disabled people. The system allows individuals and groups to play, and the prizes can be very substantial. So much so that whole villages can play, and we discovered a village that had actually won the lottery.

Odd though that concept might be, the transformative effect on this already rather pretty village was marked, with pedestrianised streets and pretty tiled squares with shaded seating areas, enhanced by the occasional piece of street art and, when we went, a fascinating produce market. The canvas-roofed stalls wound through the freshly spruced-up streets selling everything from baked goods and upmarket leatherwear to muddy carrots and fruit.

There were several stalls selling beer from microbreweries and a couple of larger makeshift bars selling the mass-produced stuff. There was even a sweet little mobile bar mounted on the back of one of those tiny Piaggio Ape toytown trucks which are little more than scooters and are more usually seen buzzing around delivering farm produce.

This conversion was masterful and a work of art. The roof, it seemed, split along the ridge and folded down, and the highly polished wooden back section unfolded to form a counter with a little sink and a cooler, beside which the artisan beers were displayed in bottles, with shelves for glasses and a till. All in miniature and all carefully decorated so that what was intended to be the old farm van became an object of great charm and a talking point all on its own.

The quality of the goods on the stalls on offer was a cut above the usual market fare, and most of the stallholders seemed to be involved in making some of the things on offer.
The bakery stalls were fascinating, with a range of bread , cakes and hot and cold items on offer. This included the little *cocas*, which they will hate me for saying, but are like mini pizzas, with all sorts of toppings. The Spanish claim the *coca* came before the pizza, but both are equally tasty (he said, to pour calm on troubled culinary waters).
There were elaborately decorated cakes, delicious looking empanadas, and sweet pastries as well.
Their customers were obviously impatient to taste these fresh goodies and weren't shy about greedily eating the produce as they shopped.

The village itself had freshly painted houses in rainbow colours with flower bedecked balconies and a handful of everyday shops. There were little street bars for when the market wasn't in town and a couple of quite expensive looking restaurants. With immaculate streets and smiling faces everywhere, winning the lottery had obviously been very good for this little place.

They also hold a *rastro* (flea) market in the original covered market area on the edge of the town, which takes place in and around a rather attractive stone built open-sided building (paid for by the lottery, perhaps), and which is very different from the stylish offerings in the other market.

This market features old paintings, items of elderly rather than antique furniture, and various curios for collectors. Last time we went, there were old vinyl records, fire guards, and car badges, as well as glassware, old plates and spoons, pepper mills, mincers, oil lamps, and frankly, anything that looked remotely old.
This was juxtaposed with a bar (inevitably), a chap selling onions and garlic, and a slightly weird looking hippy selling new 'handmade' clogs, which I strongly suspect came from China.

It's all part of the colour and vibrancy of Spain.

◆ ◆ ◆

CHAPTER 38: THAT SINKING FEELING

The town of Denia has a magnificent marina catering for huge motor cruisers and sailing boats and, around the edges, very expensive shops and restaurants to appeal to the boating types, interspersed with chandlers and boat brokerages.

It's fun to look in the windows of these places and imagine buying one of the million-pound super yachts on display. A trip to this town and a drink in one of the bars overlooking all this opulence is an occasional indulgence Bee and I allow ourselves.

We owned a boat ourselves once, many years ago, and although it was much more modest than some of the stunning gin palaces moored here, I had direct experience of what an expensive hobby boat ownership is, so I was all the more in awe of the tanned designer clad types draped on these swanky things.

Back then somebody told us that owning a boat was like standing in a cold shower tearing up ten pound notes, and we'd found that to be entirely accurate!

On one occasion we discovered there was to be a boat show at this marina, with trips and various entertainments, so we went along.

We arrived a little early, before it had properly opened, and we stood watching the small fish being chased by the slightly bigger fish (whilst keeping an eye out for the even bigger fish, just in case) in the crystal clear water from the harbour wall while we waited to go in.

'What's that?' asked Bee, pointing out across the water in between a row of boats.

It wasn't an even bigger fish, I'm glad to say. It was what appeared to be a powerboat circling slowly around a blue plastic tarpaulin in the water, with a man leaning over the side at an alarming angle and waving his arm to the pilot of the boat.
'Whatever is he doing?'

The powerboat had concealed some of the plastic but now moved out and away slightly, and we could see what was going on. As we watched, the powerboat pulled away smartly and opened up the throttles, and it became clear, as it rose slightly from the water, that it was trying to tow a boat which had sunk.

Until this point all that was visible of it was the blue folding roof over the cabin, but now, as the powerboat slewed this way and that trying to get some purchase on it, part of the superstructure of the boat itself was revealed.

It had obviously sunk on its moorings and now, lurching to one side, it started to rise from the depths. Clearly the organisers had decided that you couldn't have sunken boats in the marina during a boat show. That would create entirely the wrong image.

As the powerboat tugged with roaring engines and the stricken cruiser reluctantly unstuck itself from the bottom and was dragged, almost on its side and three quarters under water, we realised that the submerged boat was not dissimilar to the one we'd had all those years ago.

I decided that it wasn't funny at all. All these people pointing and laughing on the dock side had entirely misunderstood the seriousness of the situation. The cost of lifting the boat out, draining the water out of it, and the repairs to the no-doubt ruined fabrics, woodwork, engines and fittings would cost thousands, let alone the repair to whatever had made it sink.

I felt really sorry for the owner. That might have been us!

Bee stifled a laugh and suggested a walk through the various stalls which were now opening, displaying their boaty wares.
'Just be grateful we don't have to worry about that sort of thing happening to us anymore,' she said.

'I know it's early, but a cold beer is definitely called for,' I suggested.

I felt a little seasick after seeing such a sad spectacle.

CHAPTER 39: UP, UP, AND AWAY!

The economic situation back at home was getting worse, and in the week that Theresa May resigned, British Steel went bust and Top Shop owner Arcadia Group announced they were struggling; only W H Smith bucked the trend and made good profits. However they took some stick for charging more in airports than in high street stores for the same books, so I knew I was doing my bit to support them.

Bee and I regularly flew from the UK to Spain with Ryanair, one of the budget airlines. The cheapest way to fly with them (at the point of writing; who knows what it will be when you read this), was not to have allocated seats. Generally, once we were airborne, it was possible to swap with people so that they sat with their loved ones and I got to sit with Bee, but there were exceptions.

On one occasion I definitely got the short straw and was trapped in the middle seat by an enormous woman in the aisle seat and 'laughing boy' by the window.

As we sat down and tried to get comfortable, laughing boy, who was either drunk or high, promptly fell asleep, and I couldn't rouse him to move so that I could get to my seatbelt, which he was sitting on. In the end I had to resort to wrenching it out which elicited no response from him, other than a grunt.

While the woman on my other side struggled to force her bag down between the seat in front and her spreading frame, and was issued with an orange extension to the seat belt so she could do it up, I realised I'd forgotten to get my neck pillow out of my case which was in the locker above my head. It was much too late and too much upheaval to get it out, so my plan for a gentle snooze was off the agenda.

I did have my W H Smith magazine in the bag between my feet however, and when the seatbelt light went out, I reached for it.

The woman on my left had sort of flowed across all the available space and was now fanning herself with the in-flight magazine using the arm nearest to me. While laughing boy snored on, I timed the dive for my bag between sweeps of the giant's arm and almost got it onto my lap before the upswing caught me and I lost control of it. As it slid back into the footwell I decided the magazine could wait until later, particularly as my dive had taken me beneath my neighbour's armpit, and the fanning motion introduced me to a wave of B.O.

Laughing boy stirred in his sleep and broke wind as the smiling stewardess began serving drinks.

Perhaps a small brandy might be a good idea!

CHAPTER 40: A SAD DAY

As we look out from the balcony of our apartment towards the golf course, we can see the corner of another roof terrace on which sits an old gas barbecue. The property is occasionally occupied by two middle-aged men and must be regularly visited by a cleaner, who keeps the profusion of plants growing in pots watered.

For a couple of days Bee and I had noticed several flying, and occasionally dead bees around our property, and as the numbers increased, we wondered where they were coming from. We didn't have long to wait to find out.

On a hot afternoon as we sat digesting our lunch, we became aware of a noise. It wasn't the buzzing you associate with a solitary bee; it was a solid slightly undulating sound, and it was getting louder.

I stood up and scanned the horizon and saw a large black mass that at first I thought was smoke, over towards our neighbours' terrace. It was a swarm circling the barbecue and gradually engulfing it. There were bees everywhere, and we decided it would be prudent to go inside and close the windows. The next day there were dozens more bees all over the place, and a glance towards the neighbours' roof terrace revealed that the old barbecue was crawling with them. What was more concerning was that the windows on the floor below were open, and it was obvious that the cleaner was doing her rounds.

I hastily pulled on trainers and with my son who was staying with us at the time, rushed round to the road which sat a little below ours, where the front of the affected property was.
It was easy to spot which house it was because the front door was open, and a mop and bucket sat on the steps.

There were several bees flying round us as we approached and called out. It was clear that the Spanish lady who appeared in the doorway spoke no English, but by pointing at the flying insects, the top storey of the building, and miming, I got the message through that something was wrong.

The slightly bemused lady stepped inside and drew a mobile phone from her vast handbag.
At first I thought she was calling the police or the security guards to remove these lunatic Englishmen from the doorstep, but then she said a few rapid words as the call connected and handed me the phone.

I found myself speaking to a Spanish woman who'd obviously learned English from an American. I explained the situation which at the second attempt, she grasped and told me to hold the line. As I waited the cleaner produced a business card and pointed at the phone, and it became clear that I was speaking to the cleaner's boss who, it seemed, knew how to contact the villa owner and was calling him while I held on.

I tried to explain that perhaps a local beekeeper would be prepared to collect and relocate the hive, but I don't think I was completely understood, and eventually the voice on the other end of the phone said matters were in hand and asked me to give the phone back to the cleaner.
As I batted away a few bees and stood rather uncertainly to see what would happen next, a conversation took place in rapid Spanish, the tone of which seemed to be getting more and more panicky.

As she spoke the cleaner was rushing about gathering up her equipment and, as the call ended, she said '*Muchas gracias,*' threw the cleaning kit in the back of her car, and was gone.

We returned to our apartment, fending off bees all the while, and awaited events.

At the weekend I noticed movement on the neighbours' terrace. The bees were still there and, although not quite so evident, there were still plenty of them buzzing about.

Then I spotted what was going on. Dressed in a hoody, with the hood up, our neighbour was tentatively approaching the stricken barbecue. With what, from this distance, looked like a broom, he pushed the lid slightly open and was met with an angry cloud of bees becoming airborne. He retreated inside only to return a little later with something which was smoking, attached to the broom handle, as he held the end with the bristles.

I couldn't see what happened next, or what he was doing as he crouched down below the parapet, but a few minutes later I could guess.

The circling cloud of bees, the smoke, and the smell of burning wax quickly made it obvious that he'd turned on the gas and lit the barbecue!
This barbaric act left us with the smell of burning wax for over a week, and every day we swept up bee carcasses as the poor homeless things died all

around us.

I was told that he swore they were wasps when challenged about it later by another neighbour, but the dismay at what he'd done hung around longer than the smell, and the ruined barbecue appeared by some bins a few streets away in the dead of night a few days later.

Since then we make sure we never leave anything on our terrace when we leave the apartment, and our barbecues all live in our store.

CHAPTER 41: SELLING UP/ STAYING PUT?

How were Bee and I to solve the dilemma and decide how much of our time was to be spent in Spain?

The new deadline for leaving the EU was now 31st October 2019, but by late May, all that had happened as a result of yet more Brexit talk, was that New York had officially taken over from London as the financial centre of the world, more UK businesses had collapsed, and the major UK political parties had suffered a drubbing in the EU elections.

While the ruling Conservative party navel gazed and tried to choose a new leader, the Labour leader finally got off the fence and announced that he would, after all, back another referendum; per-

haps. In Europe, no doubt, they laughed at us as Nigel Farage, the most vitriolic 'vote leave' campaigner, jumped up and down in excitement at all the attention he was getting.
The possibility of the UK leaving the EU without a deal was back on the agenda, and business groups complained that investment was drying up because of the never-ending uncertainty.

Against that background our own worries seemed inconsequential, but like everyone else, our lives were becoming increasingly impacted by these machinations, and making decisions became harder by the day.

We knew we loved Almazara, and now that Bee had retired, we were aware we should decide how long we were going to spend there each year.
Our responsibilities in the UK had reduced dramatically since we started on this adventure, although with one son still living at home, we couldn't just sell up and go wherever we liked. David was 23 but his job, at the end of a long apprenticeship, wasn't paying him anywhere near enough to set up home on his own, whether he wanted to or not, and we had no intention of kicking him out or selling up in the UK completely in any event.

The only decision we'd come to was that there was no real pressure on us to make a decision, but comforting though that may be, it didn't really solve anything.

The idea of splitting our time 50/50 or 70/30 between Spain and the UK was attractive, but Bee had one or two conditions.
'If we were to live here for any period of time,' she said as she towelled herself off after a morning swim, 'I would want us to have our own pool, even if it was only a little one.'

There was never any problem about using the two pools we had access to, and they were always immaculately clean and fresh as the pool cleaners could be seen at work most days.

We'd met some lovely people by the pools, and it was nice to have the opportunity to bathe without the responsibility of maintenance. Even though our share of the upkeep cost was inevitably included in our maintenance charges, and we knew that sharing the cost would always be cheaper than taking on the full burden ourselves, I had to admit that having a private pool just for our own use would be nice.

'And,' I added, 'the apartment is convenient and we have great neighbours, but if we were here for a long time, it would be good to have a private garden.'

'Yes, and a roof terrace, or at least somewhere

with a view,' Bee added.
'Are you sure you don't need a tennis court and a helipad too?' I joked.

Meanwhile we'd made one decision, and that was we would fly from Norwich each time we went to Spain to avoid the cattle market that was Stansted airport. We calculated that if we chose our dates carefully, avoiding the school holidays, it was no more expensive than flying with Ryanair, and was a lot more comfortable.
Unfortunately only one airline goes from Norwich to Alicante, and Flybe was in trouble.
Matters came to a head when they announced they'd been taken over by a consortium including Virgin and had secured an injection of cash.
Inevitably the new management looked to make savings, and of course one of their early cuts was the Norwich to Alicante flights.

We had two trips bought and paid for with Flybe, which fortunately went and came back before the route closed, but in October, when we were looking forward to the next *Ruta de Tapas* and planned to visit the Alhambra, we would have to travel from a different airport.

We had a few choices; sardine style with Ryanair from Stansted, which we really didn't fancy again, or Luton, where the parking seemed very expensive and the flights were at inconvenient times, so both of those were rejected. There were lots of flights from Gatwick but for us, from darkest Norfolk, that involves a long drive and an overnight stay, so in the end we decided to give Southend airport and EasyJet a try.

Southend airport may be small and not very well equipped, but it was a relatively easy two and a half hour drive for us, and EasyJet had been less hassle than Ryanair in the past, so we booked our tickets.
The dates spanned the 31st October latest Brexit deadline date, and we'd been warned there could be disruption to flights, but we decided to take the risk because, with anything Brexit related, certainty was never going to be on the agenda, and besides, how bad could it be...

'Best check our travel insurance,' suggested Bee. 'Make sure it includes repatriation if we get stranded!'

I'd been on those Internet property sites again to see if a property with a pool was a realistic option for us and if there were any modest villas with pools that we could afford in Almazara.

We had no fixed plan but, just for a look you understand, Bee and I had driven round some of the roads near our apartment and noticed that, as well as the millionaires places, there were just a few smaller villas on the lower slopes of the mountain.

If we did ever decide to do it, however, funding such a move would be complicated and would involve selling our house in Norfolk and buying something smaller (but still big enough for David to live in with us when we were home) and selling the apartment.

Buying property in Spain is easy, but selling there is quite another matter.

Wherever you go, the *Se Vende* (For Sale) signs are much in evidence.
There are exceptions, of course, but Spanish families don't traditionally sell property, preferring to pass it on from generation to generation, so it's mostly foreigners that would-be sellers need to attract if they are wanting to sell.

It's not always understood by British people that the notion of selling and moving to something bigger, or collecting equity when downsizing, and depending on the rising property market to create (real or imagined) wealth is virtually unknown in Spain, where homes are for nesting, not investing.

The collapse of the Spanish economy, followed by successive recessions and market downturns in the wider world hasn't helped either, but there's another reason for the oversupply of property on the market.

After Franco's death, and when the economy in Spain opened up, huge amounts of development took place around the tourist hotspots particularly. The emerging property market quickly flourished as fortunes were made, and everyone tried to climb on the bandwagon of selling property to foreigners. The building boom created some appalling, as well as some very appealing property, but the financiers backing it had missed one all-important detail to ensure its success.

The concept of market research was not a well-developed art in what was, after all, an emerging economy and, depending on the theory that 'if you build it, they will come', the Spanish built, and built, and built.

Soon however the properties they were creating weren't being snapped up quite so quickly by eager buyers.
The story goes that the banks often funded developments based, not on the rate of sales, but on the rate of building, so that to get more finance the builders had to keep building, although more and more the results of their efforts sat unsold.

Eventually, of course, the bubble burst and the banks turned the taps off. The builders couldn't repay the loans so went bust, and the banks ended up holding ranks upon ranks of unsold properties with buyers becoming rarer than hens' teeth. Then house prices around Europe went into free fall as the crash bit.

Friends told us there is a small village inland from the Costas with an enormous sprawling urbanisation of nearly a thousand houses tacked onto it, which demonstrates the worst outcome of these events well.

By far the largest percentage of these houses have never been lived in, and there are streets and streets of houses completed but unsold. The swimming pools of the larger ones are dry or full of rubbish, and grass is growing on the terraces and balconies. The streetlights illuminate empty estate roads and cul-de-sacs and can be seen for miles around, but only a handful of people occupy houses there.

We were told that this particular ill-conceived estate is further hampered by the fact that the builder, anxious to draw down more and more finance from his bankers, used a fast but unreliable form of concrete construction which is notorious for problems with damp.

Sales there are also constrained by the banks, who, having finally discovered the value of market research, now take into account the number of unsold properties on an urbanisation when considering making loans, and if the percentage is too high, they don't like lending. As a result even some of the estate agents won't touch these properties.

This doomed and rather sad scheme has further problems in that the builder originally planned to build around seven hundred homes and put in infrastructure to cope with that, but ended up building nearly three hundred more, before it was discovered that the main entrance road had been built in the wrong place and the water and drainage arrangements provided didn't have the capacity to serve the development.

Years later the local council appointed a contractor to put right these mistakes, but after several attempts, the contractor said the job was impossible, and when the council tried to enforce the contract, went bust.

What it will take to resolve these problems is unclear. Millions have been invested in infrastructure and the construction of seas of deserted brand new houses, and further millions are owed in capital and interest to the funding banks, so it's not just a case of shoving a bulldozer through it and starting again.

The prices any new property could now command, post crash, might not cover the building costs, even if buyers could be found for houses on a

huge estate with no shops, play parks, or facilities of any kind, unless you travel by car, there being no public transport, the couple of miles into the original village that all this was appended to.
The situation seems hopeless. There it sits, unloved and growing weeds, while the men in suits at the banks hope it won't be them that their bosses ask to pick up the file next.

◆ ◆ ◆

We knew when we bought our place that selling in Spain wouldn't be the straightforward thing it is in the UK.
The idea was to rent it out for holidays when we got too old to use it and leave it to the kids so that the grandchildren, should any materialise, could enjoy holidays in the sun for years to come.

The idea of selling it to fund the purchase of a villa with a pool was never part of the original plan, and such a course of action was not going to be an easy option.

We thought that maybe we could find a way to keep the apartment and let it out for holidays to provide us with an income, but were concerned about the tax implications and the cost of getting it into shape for letting with all the new, and seemingly rigorously enforced rules around holiday letting that the Town Hall had recently imposed. We also wondered, if we did that, whether sufficient lettings could be achieved to make it worthwhile, and about the potential for damage and the cost of repairs.

If the apartment wasn't to be sold, we would have to sell our UK home and move to something much smaller, which might be impractical, or support the purchase by dipping into our savings, which would adversely affect the interest we relied on to top up our disappointing pensions. That in turn would make it difficult to afford to keep coming over to Spain.

The final option was to move to Spain permanently, but we weren't convinced that, after Brexit, we would be able to on terms we found acceptable, if at all, and Bee wasn't keen on that idea anyway.

What we needed was for all the third-party influences on how we managed our retirement to resolve themselves and return the same stability the UK, as a nation, had enjoyed for the last 30 or 40 years, and we looked forward to the day Brexit was finally resolved, one way or the other, so that we could plan with confidence.

CHAPTER 42: CHEEKY AND CHEEPS

Since being introduced to the *menú del día,* we'd learned a lot more about what the Spanish expect to eat, rather than what they think the Brits expect them to serve, and we'd become quite bold when we ordered our meals, no longer relying on the set menu to guide us.

We decided we were now quite comfortable in more traditional bars and restaurants and didn't need to overpay in the coastal zones or accept the tourist menus, and we decided to try to find some of the smaller places inland which the locals used.

The Spanish don't really get the concept of using a window display to attract customers, and we'd been warned that even the best places often look like transport cafés from the outside.

With its creaking hand-painted sign hanging from one nail at a crazy angle, and selection of mis-matched plastic chairs outside under grubby pro-motional umbrellas, Paco's was situated in the *campo* (countryside) well away from any main roads, down a track in amongst the orchards and vineyards, but not far as the crow flies from Al-mazara. It was as good a place to continue our search for real local cuisine as any, and Bee and I approached with confidence.

To one side of the building, under a corrugated iron roof, was a partly open-air kitchen. There was a large wood-fired oven and open charcoal grill area, blackened by years of use. What looked like blacksmiths tools hung from the canopy, and a huge pile of wood was stacked nearby. The fire was well alight, and the smell of roasting meat was mouthwatering.

Despite the heat of the day, two wizened old guys sat in long trousers, hats, and jumpers at one of the tables and nursed beers. On the other side of the terrace, beside the inevitable old television blar-ing away, and dressed almost identically, a short stooped old man unwound himself from a table and approached us with a wide grin revealing just one tooth.

He offered a greeting in *Valenciano*, and I responded in Castilian Spanish, no doubt with an appalling accent. I braced for the inevitable '*¿Qué?*' but received instead a nod and, after a moment to compose himself, '*Hola*, Eenglish, choo would lie table, no?'

I confirmed that we would and after another broad and almost toothless grin, he shepherded us to a table in the shade and flicked away invisible dust with an old threadbare tea cloth, which he drew from his back pocket.

'Eees *pollo*...um, cheek hen, OK?'
'OK.' How bad could it be?

From nowhere a young man materialised at the table and with a shy smile, offered a dog-eared piece of cardboard, which it seemed was the menu and wine list.
'You like *vino*, no? Beer, yes?'
Well, we liked both, but we ordered beer, and he drew himself up to deliver his well practiced pitch in English.

'Papa Paco, he cooker the cheeky roasted thees day. Eees cheeps too. Eees *ocho*... er...eeet euro. Ver especial and *mucha* tasty.' He made the internationally recognised finger kissing gesture.
'He cooker pizza too thees day for if you no like cheeky.' This last was delivered with an obvious lack of enthusiasm, and I guessed they would rather just sell the 'cheeky and cheeps' if they could.

Papa Paco smiled and nodded his encouragement.

We agreed that Papa Paco's chicken would be fine, and as the young man departed, the old man straightened himself and marched determinedly towards the fire, like a soldier going into battle.

You might imagine that what we would get for eeet...I mean eight...euros would be just a bland plate of chicken and chips. You couldn't be more wrong.

While the young man got our beers, a sweetly smiling little lady dressed in the traditional black appeared at the table with a large plate of cold meats, some warm fresh bread and *alioli*, and some tapenade. She said nothing but bobbed and smiled and withdrew into the main building.

The chilled bottled beers arrived with glasses and the essential knives and forks and, to my surprise, neatly folded linen napkins.

More people were arriving, and the volume level went up as they carried on inter-table conversations at full volume with much laughter. They obviously all knew one another, and the young man was joined by another waiter, presumably his brother as they were almost identical, and they were kept busy taking orders.

As far as I could tell, we were the only foreigners in

the place, and the families now joining us were obviously regulars.

There was a gruff shout from the smoky cooking area, and one of the boys rushed over and emerged with trays of steaming meat which he hurried into the main building. A few moments later he emerged with our plates, which contained huge seasoned chicken quarters, a generous portion of chips, some asparagus, and a bowl of salad with bottles of dressing.
It was utterly delicious and took us some time to finish.

Halfway through a sweating Papa Paco stood by the table.
'Eees OK, no?'

As we finished, one of the boys approached and asked if we would like *postre* (dessert), and we decided that his description of his grandmother's apple pie would do nicely.
He looked rather shamefaced as he said, '*No esta incluido; Eees €3.*'
If it was half as good as the main course, it would be a bargain.

We ordered more drinks, and by the time the dessert was eaten and we asked for the bill, the rush for Papa Paco seemed to be over, and he arrived with one of the boys holding a bottle and some glasses.

'Papa Paco would like you have drink. Eees *gratis*. You like?' he enquired.

I have no idea what the free drink was, but it went down nearly as well as the bill.

At €8 a head, including the initial drinks, plus €3 each for dessert, and a couple of euros for the other drinks, we had nothing to complain about at all, and our decision to explore the real local restaurants had got off to an excellent start. The meal, though simple, was hugely satisfying as well as great value.

The lesson we'd learned many years before, when touring Greece with empty pockets, had held good again. Getting away from the tourist areas and meeting the locals pays dividends.
We would certainly be visiting Papa Paco again, and searching out other little places off the beaten track wherever we went.

'You know, this really is great,' I grinned at Bee as I put the car away. 'We are meeting some lovely people here, and now that we've got everything fixed and working as we want it, I don't see why we would need to change anything. Brexit or not. So long as we can continue doing this, I'll be happy.'

'In that case,' said Bee with a contented smile, 'assuming Brexit doesn't completely muck up our finances and our ability to keep coming to Spain in the future, let's forget villas with pools and all that hassle, and just enjoy things as they are,' and she went to put the kettle on.

So that's what we did, and what I hoped we could continue to do for the foreseeable future.
'But of course,' said Bee, as I took the cups out onto the sunny terrace, 'I might change my mind about Spain tomorrow!'

The end... for now!

◆ ◆ ◆

So what happened next?

If you enjoyed *Spain Tomorrow*, I'm sure you'll like my forthcoming sequel, *More Spain Tomorrow*.

Here's a taster.....

More Spain Tomorrow Extract

The Spanish love a procession and, in the nearby town, despite being home to only 44,000 souls, they really went all out.

At about 8:00 in the evening, the *Festes Major* (of which more later), came to a close with the most elaborate and long procession of floats, led by a marching band. The floats themselves, creating diverse tableau from a marauding dragon to Willy Wonka's Chocolate Factory, covered a wide spectrum of themes, but all were sumptuously decorated and had obviously been the result of considerable effort.

How they were propelled was somewhat less elegant, however, with a motley collection of elderly tractors (some of which, by the look of them, had been working in the fields earlier in the day) belching out fumes and an obviously retired lorry with the cab roof cut off, its dusty instruments and steering wheel revealed. The lorry was covered in plywood and polystyrene decorations and held a throne for the fairy princess and her attendants who sat amongst the gaudily painted embellishments throwing confetti, which actually turned out to be the little paper circles you get out of office hole punches, into the crowd.

Some also towed generators to power the extensive lighting and sound systems which blared away, seemingly heedlessly competing with the marching band.

The themes included Hollywood with giant plastic Oscars amongst the grinning and highly made up children and youths riding, who were dressed as everything from Darth Vader to Mr Darcy.

A clever but sombre float warned of the impending environmental crisis with plastic bottles and other detritus used to create ocean scenes and 'The Final Countdown' on repeat on the sound system.

At the other end of the scale, a sumptuously decorated float proclaimed the glories of some subterranean world where the participants enjoyed retina-melting lighting and had wings.

This was followed by a completely bonkers four-wheel bike (hired from the seaside tourist town on the other side of the mountain for the occasion, no doubt) with an enormous speaker strapped at a precarious angle to the front and ridden by four older youths. They'd obviously been entering into the party spirit for some time as they veered madly all over the road in an effort to control the unbalanced and unwieldy contraption and its yelling, laughing, vibrating, and thumping payload.

And finally, bringing up the rear, along came the Willy Wonka float which was easily the most professional and must have been built for more than just this one event. Its glittering giant lollipops and rotating displays were manned by children who threw boiled sweets to the crowds as the lights flashed and the generator towed behind revved up to keep pace with the demand for power.

But perhaps the craziest and most enchanting part of the procession was right in the middle, where the mother and baby group, all dressed identically, came along.

This unlikely group comprised tiny babies in arms (dressed in the same outfits as their mums and older siblings), pushchairs, older children holding the hands of toddling brothers and sisters and, at their head, one smartly turned out little man, who couldn't have been more than 18 months old, marching along determinedly, dummy in mouth with his proud mum not far behind.

Just another reflection of this uninhibited fun-loving country? Well, yes and no. This was, in part at least, a religious festival to bless the coming of age of the town's youth and celebrate their patron saint.

The procession was closing the event, after the paella-cooking competition, where free food and wine were handed out, and before the fireworks, where more free food and wine were to be handed out.

This marked the close of a two-week festival which has been going on in this form since 1927. It seems the Spanish of all ages don't need any lessons in how to enjoy themselves, at all.

We were in for a fun few weeks in Spain again!

A Request

If you enjoyed this book, I would be so grateful if you left an Amazon review, even if it's simply one sentence.

THANK YOU!

Contacts and Links

EMAIL: bobable693@gmail.com

FACEBOOK: Bob Able

INSTAGRAM: BobAbleAuthor

About the Author

Bob Able has written technical papers, short stories, children's stories, and business-press items but it took an unexpected inheritance and the subsequent purchase of a holiday home in sunny Spain to inspire him to write this, the first of a series of memoirs about his adventures, mishaps, and growing enchantment with life as a part-time expat in the less touristy parts of the Costa Blanca.

When in the UK, Bob lives in darkest Norfolk with his wife, the long-suffering Bee; his family, and Barkley the dog.

Second Edition

This memoir reflects the author's recollections of experiences over a period of time. In order to preserve the anonymity of the people he writes about, some names and locations have been changed. Certain individuals are composites, and dialogue and events have been created from memory, and in some cases, compressed to facilitate a natural narrative.

Printed in Great Britain
by Amazon